PSYCHOLOGY PRACTITIONER GUIDEBOOKS

EDITORS

Arnold P. Goldstein, Syracuse University
Leonard Krasner, Stanford University & SUNY at Stony Brook
Sol L. Garfield, Washington University in St. Louis

SUICIDE RISK

Pergamon Titles of Related Interest

Becker/Heimberg/Bellack SOCIAL SKILLS TRAINING TREATMENT
FOR DEPRESSION

Feindler/Ecton ADOLESCENT ANGER CONTROL:
Cognitive-Behavioral Techniques

Goldstein/Keller AGGRESSIVE BEHAVIOR: Assessment and
Intervention

Gotlib/Colby TREATMENT OF DEPRESSION: An Interpersonal
Systems Approach

Last/Hersen HANDBOOK OF ANXIETY DISORDERS

Matson TREATING DEPRESSION IN CHILDREN
AND ADOLESCENTS

Van Hasselt/Hersen HANDBOOK OF ADOLESCENT
PSYCHOLOGY

Related Journals
(Free sample copies available upon request)

CLINICAL PSYCHOLOGY REVIEW
JOURNAL OF ANXIETY DISORDERS
JOURNAL OF CHILD PSYCHOLOGY AND PSYCHIATRY
AND ALLIED DISCIPLINES

SUICIDE RISK
Assessment and Response Guidelines

WILLIAM J. FREMOUW
West Virginia University

MARIA de PERCZEL
West Virginia University

THOMAS E. ELLIS
West Virginia University
Health Sciences Center Charleston Division

PERGAMON PRESS
Member of Maxwell Macmillan Pergamon Publishing Corporation
New York • Oxford • Beijing • Frankfurt
São Paulo • Sydney • Tokyo • Toronto

Pergamon Press Offices:

U.S.A.	Pergamon Press, Inc., Maxwell House, Fairview Park, Elmsford, New York 10523, U.S.A.
U.K.	Pergamon Press plc, Headington Hill Hall, Oxford OX3 0BW, England
PEOPLE'S REPUBLIC OF CHINA	Pergamon Press, 0909 China World Tower, No. 1 Jian Guo Men Wai Avenue, Beijing 100004, China
FEDERAL REPUBLIC OF GERMANY	Pergamon Press GmbH, Hammerweg 6, D-6242 Kronberg, Federal Republic of Germany
BRAZIL	Pergamon Editora Ltda, Rua Eça de Queiros, 346, CEP 04011, Paraiso, São Paulo, Brazil
AUSTRALIA	Pergamon Press Australia Pty Ltd., P.O. Box 544, Potts Point, NSW 2011, Australia
JAPAN	Pergamon Press, 8th Floor, Matsuoka Central Building, 1-7-1 Nishishinjuku, Shinjuku-ku, Tokyo 160, Japan
CANADA	Pergamon Press Canada Ltd., Suite 271, 253 College Street, Toronto, Ontario M5T 1R5, Canada

---

Library of Congress Cataloging in Publication Data

Fremouw, William J.
    Suicide risk : assessment and response guidelines / William J. Fremouw, Maria de Perczel, Thomas E. Ellis.
        p.   cm. -- (Psychology practitioner guidebooks)
    Includes bibliographical references.
    ISBN 0-08-036445-4 :   -- ISBN 0-08-036444-6 (pbk.) :
    1. Suicidal behavior--Risk factors. 2. Suicidal behavior--Diagnosis. I. De Perczel, Maria. II. Ellis, Thomas E. III. Title. IV. Series.
        [DNLM: 1. Suicide--prevention & control--handbooks. 2. Suicide--psychology--handbooks. HV 6545 F872s]
    RC569.F74   1990
    616.85'8445--dc20
    DNLM/DLC
    for Library of Congress   89-70960
                                                                          CIP

Printing: 2 3 4 5 6 7 8 9   Year: 1 2 3 4 5 6 7 8 9

Printed in the United States of America

The paper used in this publication meets the minimum requirements of American National Standard for Information Sciences—Permanence of Paper for Printed Library Materials, ANSI Z39.48-1984

DEDICATION

We dedicate this book to all of our past and current clients, who have taught us so much.

Contents

Preface

This book evolved from the need to provide graduate students with a concise and clear set of guidelines for use in assessing and treating potentially suicidal clients. As we began to survey the available literature for such a book, it became apparent that there were very few resources that integrated the various research and clinical findings and applied them to specific decision making for individual clients. The decision making flow chart contained in Chapter 4 is the model for suggested assessment and treatment of potentially suicidal clients. This book provides chapters discussing each of the important areas of assessment and treatment alternatives outlined by this model.

We clearly acknowledge that this book is not exhaustive in its coverage of the growing literature on suicide risk and treatment. However, we have hoped to have been selective in citing many of the most important studies in this area.

After completing this book and having shared it with several experienced colleagues, we believe that it might also be helpful to experienced clinicians to refresh themselves and to update their knowledge about the legal, clinical, and treatment issues involved in working with potentially suicidal clients. Therefore, we hope this book will be useful to both beginning mental health professionals and experienced professionals, who may find the information valuable in different ways.

Chapter 1
Suicide Risk: Historical and Legal Guidelines

Suicide, an intentional, self-inflicted death, has been documented since biblical times. In the older cultures of Greece and Rome it was often considered an honorable death. Some cultures today still consider suicide an acceptable and even venerable act. In American society, however, suicide has been viewed as an illegal act warranting criminal sanctions and by the Roman Catholic church as a mortal sin. In industrialized countries, suicide ranks among the 10 most common causes of death. Overall, suicide is the eighth or ninth leading cause of death in the United States and the third leading cause of death for younger people 15 to 24 years old (National Institute of Mental Health [NIMH], 1986). In the United States, approximately 30,000 people kill themselves annually. This is equivalent to 73 people intentionally dying by their own actions each day. In addition, at least 10 times that number of people engage in nonlethal suicidal behavior called parasuicide.

Suicide extracts a tremendous personal and financial toll. The overall rate of suicide is increasing nationally, especially among the 15 to 24 year old group (United States Monthly Vital Statistics, 1984). In addition to the lost contributions of the victims, surviving relatives and friends often carry a lifelong burden of self-doubt, guilt, or feelings of responsibility. The caregivers, therapists, clergy, or physicians are also burdened with unwelcome emotional tolls as well as potential legal liabilities for their actions or their failure to act in their treatment of the suicide victim.

The purpose of this book is to provide mental health practitioners with current information about suicide to help them make a thorough and informed assessment of a client's current risk level and needs for various life-saving interventions. This book is intended for beginning

1

mental health workers as well as experienced professionals. The information that follows will help identify ethical and legal responsibilities for these clients, the demographic factors, the clinical indicators, and the interview material that must be assessed and evaluated in determining suicide potential. In addition, the available self-report assessment measures for a suicidal assessment will be reviewed and critiqued. The unique problems of children and adolescents will be discussed in separate chapters. The reader will be guided through a flowchart for decision making that serves as a framework for the collection and integration of clinical material. Based on this heuristic model, several responses and alternatives are suggested for the management of people at various levels of suicidal risk.

We hope that if a professional uses the following suggestions then he or she will have exercised the highest standards of professional judgment that would help reduce the chance of misevaluating and mistreating the potentially suicidal person. Maintaining the highest standards of assessment practice can better serve and protect our clients, and also can protect us from potential legal liabilities. The remainder of this chapter will address the ethical and legal obligations and standards that are applied to mental health professionals.

ETHICAL AND PROFESSIONAL STANDARDS

Each of the major helping mental health professions—psychiatry, psychology, and social work—have ethical standards that guide professional practices. Whether or not explicitly stated, the protection of human life from self-destruction is an implicit value and goal of each profession. This value is apparent in the ethical standards for disclosing personal and private information about a client.

These professions all recognize the importance of maintaining a confidential relationship with clients. However, this respect for confidentiality is not considered more important ethically than responsible actions to protect a client or others from harm. Across these professions, a similar ethical obligation to protect clients from harm is clear. The American Psychiatric Association's *Principles of Medical Ethics* (1981) states that "Psychiatrists at times may find it necessary, in order to *protect the patient or community from imminent danger* [italics added], to reveal confidential information disclosed by the patient." Similarly, the National Association of Social Workers' *Standards for the Private Practice of Clinical Social Work* (1981) says that "the clinical social worker in private practice may find it necessary to reveal confidential information disclosed by the patient to *protect the patient or the community from imminent danger* [italics added]." The American Psychological Association's *Ethical Principles for Psychologists* (1981) identifies an ethical "obligation to respect the confidentiality of information obtained from persons in the course of their work as psychologists. They reveal such information to others only with the consent of the person or the person's legal representative, except in those circumstances in which *not to do so would result in clear danger to the person or to others* [italics added]." Finally, the American Association of Marriage and Family Therapy's *Code of Professional Ethics* (n.d.) also protects the confidentiality of clients "unless there is *clear and immediate danger to an individual or to society* [italics added]." Thus, according to these standards, therapists must act to disclose information to protect a client or others when clear or imminent danger exists. Regardless of a client's wishes or protests, the presence of clear or imminent danger ethically nullifies the general guideline of maintaining information in confidence. This consistent ethical obligation illustrates the value to prevent the loss of life or danger to our clients or others. While some philosophers may endorse some forms of suicide, such as among the terminally ill or chronically suffering, there is no debate or disagreement among the mental health community that acting to preserve life is an ethical responsibility and an activity consistent with the ethical values in the helping professions.

LEGAL STANDARDS

Malpractice

In addition to ethical guidelines developed by the professions, legal standards exist that create a clear obligation for therapists when working with clients in clear or imminent danger. Failure to fulfill any of these established ethical or legal duties is potential grounds for a malpractice suit against the therapist by the client's surviving family or a client who has survived a suicide attempt. Historically, negligence leading to the suicide of a client is the fourth most common cause of malpractice claims against psychotherapists (Schwitzgebel & Schwitzgebel, 1980) and accounts for approximately 15% of psychiatric malpractice cases (Hogan, 1979). Faulty services, wrongful commitment, and slander-libel were the three most common causes of claim.

More recently, the American Psychological Association (APA) Insurance Trust studied the number and type of cases against psychologists from 1976 to 1986. The death of a client accounted for 10.5% of the cases against psychologists during these 10 years. This is also the fourth most common cause of legal action after sexual impropriety, incorrect treatment, and loss from an evaluation. Interestingly, failure to warn a potential victim of a client was grounds for only 6% of the cases. There-fore, the very visible Tarasoff warning (to be discussed later in this chapter) accounted for approximately one half of the court cases against psychologists as compared with the failure to prevent the suicide of a client. Pope (1986) analyzed the APA insurance data from this period and found that the death of a client was the third most costly settle-ment of successful cases against psychologists after sexual improprie-ties and incorrect treatment. The failure to warn potential victims, de-spite widespread professional concern, only ranked as the seventh most costly for malpractice damage. Overall, the death of a client has a greater frequency of claims and higher cost of malpractice actions than the fail-ure to warn cases.

Requirements for Malpractice

If a patient commits suicide or injures his or herself while under the care of a therapist, the therapist may be liable for monetary damages under malpractice proceedings. Malpractice is a form of civil court ac-tion under tort law in which individuals are allowed to seek compen-sation from others for actions or omissions that produce the damages. Torts are categorized into unintentional and intentional types. Unin-tentional torts are based on the concept of negligence. Negligence ex-ists when a person is reckless or fails to use reasonable measures or actions to ensure that others are not harmed. Intentional torts, in con-trast, refer to deliberate actions by an individual, such as battery, that are intended to harm another. Malpractice is a type of negligence or unintentional tort when applied to professional actions. (For an excel-lent review of this subject see Cohen, 1979.)

Four elements must exist for a successful claim of malpractice. First, the defendant must have a professional duty to the plaintiff. A thera-pist who has met someone at a party but has never opened a case for that person does not have a professional duty since a professional re-lationship was never consummated. However, a client, after requesting and receiving a professional appointment, has established a profes-sional relationship with the therapist. Once started, the therapist has the duty to exercise accepted professional standards with that client until the case is closed by mutual agreement or the client is transferred to another professional.

Second, if a professional duty exists between the therapist and client, the therapist must have violated that duty by either an act of omission or commission. Failure to adequately assess the suicide risk by not ap-plying current professional standards would be an act of omission. Challenging a manipulative client to "go ahead and do it," with the result of self-destructive behavior, could be an act of commission. The definition of duty in terms of current reasonable professional practice is an area for debate. The definition of reasonable professional care has evolved from local standards of practice (i.e., what is done in the geographic area) to a national standard of accepted practice for professionals of similar orientation across the nation. This standard for professional care reflects the current professional research and practice of a reasonable and prudent professional.

Third, if a professional duty is violated, it must be the "proximate cause of an injury." Proximate cause is the legal cause considered sufficient for the injury to occur. Suicide can have a multitude of causes or factors. The proximate cause is the *one* cause that led directly to the injury or death and is legally considered "but for this cause this injury would have not occurred." Other factors may be considered legally as remote causes that had some impact on the ultimate outcome but were not the proximate or "but for" cause. Failure to assess the suicide risk of a patient or failure to take adequate precautions have been found to be proximate causes of suicidal acts.

The fourth element requires that the injury be recognized as worthy of compensation. The death of a human being is considered a legally protected interest and worthy of compensation. However, psychological injuries such as emotional distress, guilt by survivors, or mistrust by survivors vary from state to state in terms of their legitimacy for compensation (Cohen, 1979).

In summary, for a successful malpractice suit the plaintiff must demonstrate *each* of the following elements:

1. A professional duty existed between the therapist and client.
2. The therapist violated this duty by either acts of omission or commission relative to accepted national standards for reasonable professional care.
3. This violation of duty was the "proximate cause" of an injury.
4. This injury is a legitimate claim for compensation.

In general, liability for a suicidal client may arise from (a) a failure to recognize acceptable signals for a suicide risk or (b) failure to take proper action when risk is identified.

Abandoning a client by failing to fulfill professionally dictated responsibilities, such as not returning emergency calls, not providing back up services, or not initiating new patient treatment where needed, may also be a cause of liability and falls under failure to take proper action.

Danger to others. The courts do not generally hold that adults should be responsible for preventing other adults from harming themselves. For example, we are not legally obligated to stop a neighbor from jumping off a high building. However, psychiatric patients, because of their disorders, may have less control over their actions or thought processes in the eyes of the law. Therapists, by virtue of their special relationship with their clients, are given the additional responsibility to identify and prevent the dangerous actions of their clients.

A famous case of this type occurred in California. Prosenjit Poddar, an Indian graduate student at the University of California, told his psychologist that he had fantasies of harming and maybe even killing Tatiana Tarasoff, an American girl he had dated casually. Alarmed by the potential danger to Ms. Tarasoff, the therapist unsuccessfully attempted to have Poddar civilly committed. The university police questioned him and warned him to avoid Ms. Tarasoff but no other action was taken. Poddar quit treatment and a few months later stabbed her to death.

The victim's family sued for civil damages alleging that the police and therapist had been negligent in failing to warn their daughter and in failing to confine Poddar. After the case was dismissed by a lower court, the California Supreme Court in 1974 found for the family. In this landmark decision of *Tarasoff v. Board of Regents of the University of California*, the court created a duty for therapists to warn potential victims of clients when a warning is needed to avert danger arising from the psychological condition of the patient.

This decision created a professional controversy over the potentially harmful effect on the therapeutic relationship and the duty to warn potential victims. The California Supreme Court, after receiving briefs from the American Psychiatric Association, reheard the case and issued a revised ruling in 1976 that broadened the therapist's duty from just warning the potential victim to taking appropriate action to protect the potential victim. The court said, "when a therapist determines or pursuant to the standard of his profession should determine that his patient presents a serious danger of violence to another, he incurs an obligation to use reasonable care to protect the intended victim against such danger. The discharge of the duty . . . may call for him to warn the intended victim or others likely to apprise the intended victim of danger, to notify the police, or take whatever steps are reasonably necessary under the circumstances" (p. 346).

Although this case only has direct jurisdiction in California, courts in at least 12 states and several federal jurisdictions have adopted a similar therapist duty to protect potential victims of a patient. The issues of the ease of identifying the potential victim and the imminence of danger to the potential victim vary from ruling to ruling and are still evolving (Beck, 1987).

In the midst of concern about the Tarasoff ruling and its effect on therapists' ability to have confidential relationships with clients, the State of Ohio passed legislation, S.B-156, that negated the Tarasoff obligation. In this legislation, therapists are absolved from a duty to protect potential victims and are given immunity from potential damages. Although not as broad as Ohio's immunity law, California, Minnesota, Colorado, Kentucky, Louisiana, and New Hampshire have passed legislation to limit the responsibility of therapists to act only in situations in which actual knowledge exists of danger to a specific individual (Fulero, 1988). These recent laws may mark a shift in legal duties toward further circumscribing the duties of therapists away from the extreme responsibility of having to foresee potential danger to any or all potential victims of each of their clients.

Danger to self. The Tarasoff case is often thought of as providing legal precedence for the management of suicidal clients. However, it explicitly only addresses the obligations of therapists to protect others from the harm of their individual clients. The therapists' duty to protect their own clients from self-destruction exists outside of the Tarasoff rulings and subsequent decisions or legislative changes such as in Ohio and California.

Cases involving client suicide generally fit one of three basic scenarios: (a) a patient commits suicide while hospitalized; (b) a recently discharged psychiatric patient commits suicide, or (c) an outpatient, never hospitalized, commits suicide while under a therapist's care (Klein & Glover, 1983). Psychiatrists, because they are legally responsible for inpatient care, are generally the defendants in the first two types of cases, but all therapists are potential defendants in the outpatient situations.

Because of the difficulty in predicting future patient behavior, the courts have often upheld a psychiatrist's decision if reasonable judgment was demonstrated, even if death occurred. For example, in *Topel v. Long Island Jewish Medical Center* (1981), a suicidal patient killed himself while hospitalized, although he was being checked every 15 minutes as a suicide precaution. The New York Court of Appeals reversed an initial award of damages to the widow, upholding the psychiatrist's action as showing reasonable judgment about the risks and benefit of the hospital program.

However, psychiatrists have been found liable when reasonable judgment and precautions were not demonstrated with hospitalized patients. In *Meier v. Ross General Hospital* (1968), a psychiatrist was liable for the death of a suicidal patient who jumped from a hospital window. The patient had been allowed access to an openable, second story window despite a previous suicide attempt. The court found that the psychiatrist had failed to assess adequately the risk of suicide and had failed to take reasonable actions to prevent a future attempt. A more recent case of *Texarkana Memorial Hospital, Inc. v. Firth* (1988) had a similar outcome. The family of a 33-year-old woman who was admitted for suicidal risk and psychosis was awarded over $950,000 for gross negligence by the hospital. When she was admitted the locked ward had no empty beds. To lower her risk of suicide, she was sedated but placed in an open ward with no special suicidal precautions. Upon awakening, she jumped to her death. A court of appeals affirmed the award and finding of gross negligence by the hospital for failure to take reasonable steps to prevent this death. Failure to take appropriate precautions was also the basis of the *Abille v. United States* (1980). A psychiatrist was found liable when a patient committed suicide after being transferred from suicide status to a lower level of precaution without adequate medical notes to explain the rationale for such an important decision. The court implied that if good notes demonstrating a reasonable, thoughtful decision had been kept as required by hospital policy, then the psychiatrist may not have been found responsible for the patient's death. However, in the absence of notes, a breach of duty and failure to follow professional standards had occurred.

When a recently discharged patient attempts or commits suicide, the courts assess (a) whether an appropriate assessment of the potential risk was made and (b) whether reasonable judgment was exercised in the decision to discharge the patient. In *Bell v. New York City Health and Hospital Corporation* (1982), the psychiatrist was found liable for injuries suffered in a suicide attempt by a delusional patient because the defendant had not assessed the patient's delusional beliefs or prior behavior before discharging the patient. When the psychiatrist has made a reasonable assessment and no longer believes that a risk of danger exists, he is not held responsible for the postdischarge death of the patient. For example, in *Johnson v. United States* (1981) and *Paradies v. Benedictine Hospital* (1980), the courts did not find the psychiatrists responsible for the postdischarge suicides of their patients because the psychiatrists had assessed the patients and had reasonably concluded that the benefits of release outweighed the potential risks of danger. In *Johnson,* the court observed that "accurate predictions of dangerous behavior, and particularly of suicide and homicide, are almost never possible" (p. 1293).

Although the courts do not demand perfect predictive abilities, they do expect clients with suicide risk to have an appropriate assessment of their risk and to receive reasonable and documented treatment programs. The cases of *Bell, Meier,* and *Abille* are examples of psychiatrists' failure to meet these two standards.

Suicide by outpatients also raises the two issues of (a) whether the therapist properly assessed the potential suicide risk and (b) if recognized, whether the therapist took appropriate actions to lessen the risk. In contrast with hospitalized treatment, outpatient treatment raises new challenges in exercising appropriate actions to lessen the potential risk. A therapist does not have the benefit of 24-hour observations, locked wards, and even seclusion cells to prevent suicidal acts. In outpatient care, more frequent sessions, daily phone calls, increased family involvement, and/or medications are often used but do not offer the same degree of control over suicidal patients as is available in a hospital setting. Because therapists have less control over an outpatient than an inpatient, outpatient therapists have not been held as responsible for their patients' actions as therapists of inpatients. For example, in *Speer v. United States* (1981), the court stated that a psychiatrist's duty to outpatients is less than the responsibilities to inpatients. Although *Bellah v. Greenson*, (1978) acknowledged a higher duty to prevent suicide in a hospital setting, the court did reassert a therapist's responsibility to foresee potential suicide risk and to take reasonable preventive measures for outpatients. The court did not require the therapist to warn the family of the potential risk to their daughter. Unlike the earlier Tarasoff duty to warn obligation, the court balanced the patient's right to confidentiality against the risk of self-harm and chose not to require the therapist to warn others. Instead, the court left the appropriate action to prevent suicide to professional judgment.

Overall, the malpractice cases involving the suicide of a client have supported the professionals if a proper assessment had been completed—in *Johnson v. United States* (1981), for example—and if reasonable documented judgment had been exercised in the treatment decisions about someone at risk for suicide, such as in *Topel v. Long Island Jewish Medical Center* (1981). With outpatients, a Tarasoff type of duty to warn relatives of potential suicide risk is not current case law (*Bellah v. Greenson*, 1978), but remains one of several appropriate options that should be seriously considered. Chapter 8 includes discussion on many additional treatment options to help clients who are at risk.

Reducing the Risk of Malpractice

This book is designed to increase professional awareness of characteristics of suicidal clients and provide concrete suggestions for the management of suicidal clients. Obtaining this type of knowledge is the first step toward both increasing the effectiveness of treatment of clients as well as decreasing the risk of professional liability. However, knowledge and application of these principles alone is not enough. In the unfortunate case of an unavoidable suicide, a therapist's retrospective statements that she or he had exercised reasonable concern, caution, and assessment of a client does not protect him or her unless there are adequate records reflecting the series of careful professional judgments and data collection steps. Considering the demographic characteristics, weighing the clinical risk factors, eliciting critical interview material, and administering a thorough battery of self-report measures does not alone ensure adequate professional practice. All of these steps must be documented at the time of their completion. Ongoing record keeping, not after-the-fact notes, are one of the most important steps toward reducing the risk of malpractice suits.

Any therapist, regardless of how competent, successful, and skilled, may lose a client through suicide. What will distinguish this therapist from another who was clearly negligent, careless, and indifferent to her or his client's suicidal state is the presence of a well-documented, thorough clinical record.

As Tarasoff cases have evolved, the courts have not required that therapists be able to predict future behavior with certainty. Social scientists have educated the court for decades about the great difficulty in predicting specific acts from specific people. The Supreme Court has acknowledged that psychiatrists and psychologists are accurate in less than one of three predictions of violent behavior (*Barefoot v. Estelle*, 1983). The courts have found, however, that therapists must function at an acceptable level of professional practice and must take reasonable steps to obtain and analyze important data about their clients. Failure to do an adequate assessment cannot be excused by the imprecision of our disciplines. If, however, after adequate assessment our predictions are occasionally wrong, then at least we have demonstrated reasonable professional judgment and we would probably not be considered negligent.

SUMMARY

In summary, therapists have both an ethical and legal responsibility to adequately assess potential suicide risk and to act to prevent self-injurious acts. This responsibility is independent of the Tarasoff case laws and controversy. Successful claims of malpractice can arise from the therapist's failure either to assess or to take adequate steps to prevent suicidal acts. Competent, professional treatment requires knowledge and the ability to integrate a variety of demographic, clinical, and test data to make an informed professional decision as to proper management of the client. This must be accompanied by a thorough record of these data and the treatment decision.

Chapter 2
Conceptions and Misconceptions of Suicide: A Historical Perspective

An adequate understanding of suicidal behavior requires both a cultural and historical perspective. Suicide is a complex, multidimensional phenomenon with a long history and with many meanings through the ages and across cultures. Suicide is also subject to numerous misconceptions, both among members of the lay public and within the professional community. In this chapter we will explore suicide as a social phenomenon, tracing both its place in history and its various social ramifications. We will then turn to some myths and facts about suicide, juxtaposing some of the more common misconceptions of suicide with the current state of scientific and clinical knowledge.

SUICIDE THROUGH THE AGES

The history of suicide goes back almost as far as recorded history itself. As early as the third millenium B.C., ancient Egyptian history reveals accounts of completed suicides, suicide notes, and even suicide threats to obtain sympathetic treatment from significant others (Hankoff, 1979). We even find in this literature a philosophical debate between an unhappy man and his soul on the various implications of taking one's own life (Hankoff, 1979, p. 26).

Flavius Josephus, a Jewish-leader-turned-Roman-historian who lived in the first century A.D., wrote extensively about suicide. He wrote accounts of at least 24 incidents of both individual and mass suicides spanning a period from 1500 B.C. to 73 A.D. Included was the famous incident at Masada wherein, after a 3 year defense of their fortress against the Romans, 960 soldiers killed themselves rather than be subjected to defeat, capture, or possible execution.

Attitudes toward suicide have varied through the ages, from implicit approval through neutral tolerance to total condemnation. Ancient Egyptians, because they saw death only as passage to another state of being, viewed suicide rather neutrally. Since they believed that the dead, no less than the living, needed to be fed, clothed, and made comfortable, they were concerned less with survival than with ensuring that they be properly buried and cared for after death.

At the opposite end of the spectrum were the ancient Judaic' prohibitions against suicide. Although the Bible contains no explicit condemnation of suicide, Judaism strongly forbade self-destruction; elements of this prohibition survive to this day in contemporary Judaism, Christianity, and Islam (Hankoff, 1979).

Classical Romans placed a rather low premium on human life, and suicide was viewed neutrally, or even positively when used by a man to save face or when chosen by a prisoner as an alternative to execution for capital crimes. Ironically, Christians during this period, while condemning suicide among pagans, eagerly met their deaths at the hands of the Romans because of their expectation of bliss in heaven. Church leaders became increasingly concerned about excessive martyrdom until, in the fifth century, A.D., St. Augustine denounced suicide as equivalent to murder and therefore a violation of the Fifth Commandment that "thou shalt not kill." At one point, the Catholic church enacted sanctions against suicide attempters, completers, and survivors that included defamation and even torture (Shneidman, 1976).

Sanctions against suicide were continued and intensified during the Middle Ages. In England, committing suicide meant that the family lost inheritance of the deceased's possessions, and committing suicide to avoid criminal prosecution meant forfeiting land ownership as well. However, perhaps for the first time, exceptions were made in cases of suicide related to insanity. As late as the 18th and early 19th centuries, however, penalties for suicide included defiling the corpse in various ways. The French dragged the body through the streets and hung it at a gallows or threw it into a sewer; the English pounded a stake through the heart and buried the corpse in an unmarked grave at a crossroads (Rosen, 1975).

Perhaps in part as a reaction to these extreme measures, 18th century philosophers began for the first time to discuss suicide apart from the concept of sin or crime (Shneidman, 1976). David Hume contended that suicide was not a violation of our duties to God or society and that a person in fact should end his or her life when it became an excessive burden. Rousseau, consistent with his role as social critic, shifted the blame for suicide from the individual to society (Shneidman, 1976).

Modern times have seen a steady erosion of legal sanctions against suicide. In the United States, 45 states exclude suicide from their criminal codes; the other five define it as a crime but not punishable if accomplished (Perr, 1979). Internationally, the most liberal view of suicide is probably in Holland, where physician-assisted euthanasia is legal in cases of terminal illness. Religious practices vary, but the current Catholic view that suicide is usually the result of mental illness and therefore not the responsibility of the victim (Cassidy & Russo, 1979) seems representative.

MYTHS AND MISCONCEPTIONS
ABOUT SUICIDE

As might be expected from the varied and sometimes extreme attitudes toward suicide, objective facts about suicidal behavior have often been obscured by myths and misunderstandings. This is caused not only by the emotional nature of the subject matter, but also because in many respects suicide research is still in its infancy. In this section we will list some of the more common misunderstandings of suicide, first among the lay public and then within the professional community, and in each case present information more consistent with current research and our clinical experience. We hope that this information will be used for purposes of both public education and as a guide to clinical intervention.

Common Public Misconceptions
About Suicide

People often commit suicide without warning—"out of the blue." This is perhaps the most common error made in media accounts of suicides, particularly highly publicized and sensationalized ones. Television reporters, for example, sometimes interview neighbors or school teachers who express dismay that this "boy next door" would do such a thing. In reality, people who engage in suicidal behavior, especially those who complete suicide, generally have given multiple obvious or subtle indications of distress, such as saying good-byes or putting their affairs in order. Furthermore, studies show that suicidal persons generally have had long histories of emotional maladjustment and maladaptive behavior. Maris (1981) coined the term "suicidal careers" to describe this process. His important study showed that suicidal persons were more likely than comparison groups to have been socially isolated, to have had problems with alcohol, to have had a major mental disorder, and to have failed to master major developmental life tasks. Interestingly, most of the correlates of completed suicide were equally or even more likely to predict nonfatal suicide attempts.

Sometimes a minor event such as a poor test grade can push an otherwise normal person to commit suicide. This belief is reflected both in oversimplified media accounts of suicide ("Youth Commits Suicide After Listening to Rock Music") and in the tendency of survivors to worry that something they said or did might have pushed the victim "over the edge." This view overlooks the pivotal role of cognitive mediation in determining coping responses to life events. Research has shown that, in addition to manifesting long-term adjustment problems, suicidal persons also have characteristic cognitive patterns such as rigid thinking, deficient problem-solving skills, and irrational beliefs that predispose them to respond to stressful events with maladaptive behaviors (Ellis, 1986). Cognitive characteristics of suicidal persons will be discussed more fully in Chapter 10.

Only crazy people commit suicide. At the opposite extreme from the "it could happen to anyone" belief is the idea that suicidal behavior is de facto evidence of insanity. While suicide is not infrequently committed by persons with schizophrenia or psychotic depression, the majority of suicidal acts are committed by individuals without psychotic processes. What is less clear is to what extent "rational" suicide is possible, especially in light of the considerable evidence of psychopathology and cognitive impairments among suicidal persons. This is an area of ongoing controversy, with reputable authors arguing both sides of the issue (e.g., Maris, 1983; Szasz, 1986).

If a person committed suicide, his or her situation was probably so bad that death was the best solution. This belief is based for the most part on a value judgment of what makes a life worth living. To say that a person's life is no longer worth living is to presume to know the value of a human life. For example, in medical settings it is not unusual to hear medical students and residents comment that suicide would be "understandable" or perhaps reasonable for patients with terminal illnesses. However, at least one study (Brown, Henteleff, Barakat, & Rowe, 1986) showed that patients with terminal illnesses were rarely suicidal and that those patients who did become suicidal were also clinically depressed. On the other hand, evidence also shows that suicide rates among persons suffering from AIDS is many times higher than the general population (Marzuk et al., 1988). While it may be impossible to settle the rationality issue empirically, most clinicians are well aware that the life circumstances of suicidal people, while often bad, are survived by most people in similar circumstances.

People who threaten suicide don't do it. This belief probably stems from a rather common assumption that suicidal communication is intended to "get attention" or to manipulate others, and that people who are "really serious" would just proceed quietly with their plans. While we do not know the percentage of suicide threateners who actually carry through on their threats, several studies have shown no fewer than two thirds of suicide victims to have communicated their intentions at some point before committing suicide (Murphy, 1985).

People who really want to die will find a way; it won't help to try to stop them. We know from post-mortem studies that the vast majority of people who kill themselves were suffering from depression, schizophrenia, or alcoholism at the time of their deaths. All these are highly treatable illnesses, and symptom relief almost always eliminates the wish and the motive for suicide. Furthermore, the impulse to commit suicide is generally an acute, transient experience that often passes if delayed, with or without treatment. Finally, the expression "people who really want to die" is largely misconceived. Most suicidal people are highly ambivalent about suicide—at the same time that they desire death they generally also wish desperately to be rescued so that they can have another chance at life.

The tendency toward suicide is inherited and passed from generation to generation. In one sense, this statement has validity; but it can also be misconstrued. Twin adoption studies have suggested that suicide may have some genetic component beyond that associated with depression, alcoholism, and schizophrenia. However, the issue is far from resolved, since these studies are subject to criticism on methodological grounds (Murphy, 1985). Moreover, suicidal behavior can also be "transmitted" through modeling by family members. We also know that suicide occurs in individuals with no family history of suicide. So, at best this statement is only partially true and must not be used as a way of saying that suicidal people cannot be helped.

One should not try to discuss suicide with depressed people; it might give them the idea or upset them enough to "push them over the edge." Suicide is seldom a novel idea to depressed people, and they are commonly greatly relieved to be given "permission" to talk about it. The greater risk is that the topic be passed over because the depressed person considers suicide too "shameful" to mention. This can result in an even greater sense of isolation. At worst, inquiring about suicidal thoughts can produce a puzzled look or irritation from someone who is not to the point of being suicidal; at best, it can demystify a dark secret and lead to the depressed person getting the help he or she needs.

The great majority of suicides are among minority groups from lower socioeconomic classes; the age group at highest risk these days is young people. Whites have suicide rates from 50% to 100% higher than African-Americans and Hispanics. One place where the gap closes is among young African-American males, whose suicide rate approaches that of young white males. The age group at highest risk for suicide continues to be the elderly—white males over age 50 comprise 10% of the population but account for 30% of suicides (Hendin, 1982). However, suicide among young persons nearly tripled between 1950 and 1980, from 4.5 per 100,000 to 12.3 per 100,000, close to the overall population rate (Centers for Disease Control, 1986). The increase seems to have leveled off in recent years, although it may still be climbing among 15- to 19-year-olds (Suicide Research Digest, 1988). Regarding social class, studies indicate lower rates in the middle ranges and higher rates in higher classes and the unskilled working classes, as well as among the unemployed (Kreitman, 1981).

Suicides occur in greatest numbers around Christmas and Thanksgiving. Christmas and Thanksgiving are actually the least risky of the six major U.S. holidays (of course, this does not change the fact that many individuals may have difficulty with these holidays). While the incidence of suicide in the United States is relatively consistent throughout the year, it is lowest during the winter months and highest in the spring (Centers for Disease Control, 1985). Reasons for seasonal variations in suicide (and homicide) rates have not been fully explained.

Common Professional Misconceptions About Suicide

Improvement following a suicidal crisis means the suicide risk is over. Clinicians must interpret signs of improvement in suicidal patients cautiously. Lessening of depressive symptoms may mean that the depression is lifting, but may also mean that the patient feels a sense of relief from having finally made the decision to end his or her life. Moreover, many of the psychological liabilities that cause some people to respond to stress with suicidal thinking have trait-like qualities and may resurface when stress increases. For these reasons, the clinician is well-advised to thoroughly pursue inquiry into possible suicidal thinking, even though overt symptoms have lifted (and even though the patient may wish to move on to other topics).

If someone survives a suicide attempt, he or she must have been doing it as a manipulation. This is a relatively common reaction to parasuicide and is a variant on the idea that people who "really" want to kill themselves will find a way to do so. In reality, there are numerous possible motives behind suicidal behavior, and people almost always have more than one reason. Nonfatal self-destructive behavior may be a form of problem-solving, a cry for help, a means of self-punishment, or a way of expressing anger or pain. Calling parasuicide "manipulation" is a tautological label ("This person engaged in nonfatal behavior because he or she wanted to manipulate; I know it was manipulative behavior because it was nonfatal"); this circular logic has no explanatory value. A preferable course is to abstain from perjorative labeling and seek an explanation in terms of the problem the individual was trying to solve, albeit maladaptively, through self-destructive behavior.

One should not reinforce pathological behavior by attending to vague references to suicide. Here, again, it is important for the clinician not to allow fear of manipulation to lead to overlooking real messages of suicidal intent. Suicidal persons can be expected to be both ambivalent and perhaps somewhat ashamed of their suicidal ideas since suicide is generally considered socially undesirable behavior. The suicidal individual's ambivalence produces both a desire to avoid detection and interference and a simultaneous wish to be rescued. This can lead to vague references to suicide and a more-or-less fatalistic attitude about the therapist's picking up on clues. Moreover, from a behavioral standpoint, an excellent way to diminish hinting of suicide as a way of getting attention might be to "talk it to death" each time the patient brings it up.

Most people who parasuicide once can be expected to make multiple attempts; most people who kill themselves usually have made multiple previous nonlethal attempts. Actually, most people's first suicide attempt is also their last; 66% of attempters never make another attempt. Thus, only a minority of suicidal people have multiple episodes of suicidal behavior. Moreover, about half of suicide fatalities have made no previous attempts. However, having made an attempt, attempters as a group are at a 15% to 20% lifetime risk for eventual death by suicide. Both of these facts underscore the potential value of effective crisis intervention and prevention of both fatal and nonfatal suicide attempts.

If a person is talking to a therapist about suicide, he or she probably is not going to do it. A person truly intent on suicide is likely to hide it from people who might stop him or her. As many as 80% of people who ultimately kill themselves have communicated their intentions to someone (Berman, 1975). Three fourths visit a physician within 4 months, half within 1 month, of taking their lives (Suicide: Part 1, 1986). As a rule, people do talk about their intentions (or fears) of committing suicide; talking about suicidal thoughts is an indication of higher, not lower, risk.

Suicide is to be expected in cases of severe hardship, especially in persons with terminal illness. Often, statements such as this are an indication of the speaker's belief that he or she could not bear to experience similar hardship. In reality, experience shows that human beings are capable of enduring tremendous adversity and still maintain a fierce determination to live. At least one study (Brown et al., 1986) has shown that, even in cases of incurable cancer, the great majority of victims wished to live as long as possible. The few who had contemplated suicide were found to be suffering from clinical depression, a treatable suicide risk factor in itself.

The main factor in suicide is psychopathology; suicidal people have about the same level of life stress as nonsuicidal people. While it is true that some people respond with suicidal acts to situations that others would cope with, it is also known that stresses are more frequent and more severe, on the average, in the lives of persons who become suicidal (e.g., Paykel, 1979; Linehan, 1981). This finding is not necessarily in conflict with the study described above if one considers the possibility that being suicidal represents an interaction between high stress levels and inadequate coping skills (Schotte & Clum, 1987).

Suicide ideators, attempters, and completers all are from the same psychiatric population, with a continuum of severity in the direction of completers. While considerable overlap exists between populations, people who commit suicide and those with nonfatal attempts have quite different modal profiles. Among parasuicides, females outnumber males three to one. They tend to be younger than completed suicides and typically use low lethality methods such as wrist-cutting and nonlethal drug overdoses. On the other hand, among completed suicides, male suicides outnumber female suicides by almost three to one. In contrast to personality disorders found more typically among parasuicides, affective and substance use disorders predominate among suicides. As would be expected, methods used tend to be violent and lethal and include gunshot, hanging, and jumping. When they survive, persons from this population tend to be disappointed that they survived and angry at their rescuers. In contrast, attempters tend to express relief that they are still alive and show improvement relatively quickly after intervention.

A person who makes a non–life-endangering attempt or who makes an attempt with a high chance of rescue must not have been serious about dying and is not at high risk for suicide. A common error among clinicians is to confuse suicide lethality with suicidal intent, such that it is assumed that minor physical harm equates with minimal intent to die. This assumes that most people are sophisticated in their understanding of drug dosages and anatomy. Human intentions are subtle and complex and must be inferred with caution and with information from a variety of sources. Variables such as method used, the amount of physical harm done, treatment required, the location, and probability of rescue, among others, must be considered (Weissman & Worden, 1972).

There are two groups of suicidal patients: those who are serious about dying and those who are trying to manipulate somebody. The clinician attempting to dichotomize patients into these groups risks being guilty of the same black-and-white thinking that creates problems for many clients. To avoid oversimplification, clinicians must realize that suicidal people are rarely single-minded in their intentions. Suicidally depressed patients typically hold out some hope of being rescued; multiple attempters, particularly those with borderline personality disorders, generally acknowledge some constant desire to cease living. Understanding this coexistence of wishes may be crucial to helping people in either category.

SUMMARY

Suicide has been a part of civilization since biblical times. Depending on the time and culture, suicidal behavior has been accepted or condemned, and many myths about suicidal people have evolved. These myths, without empirical foundation, have perpetuated many of the prejudices about suicidal people that have interfered with effective identification and prevention of suicidal behavior. Appropriate and effective intervention requires recognizing these myths and knowing the factual alternatives.

Chapter 3
Epidemiology of Suicide

Competent assessment and treatment of suicidal or potentially suicidal clients requires knowledge that extends beyond the unique characteristics of the individual to patterns that exist in social systems. The purpose of epidemiology is to identify such patterns in various segments of society, defined according to age, gender, geographic location, environmental conditions, or other variables.

Discussions of suicide typically begin with, or at least include, an assortment of statistics, which may be met by readers with varying degrees of tolerance or impatience. Therapists sometimes fail to see any particular relevance of such numbers to their practical dilemmas concerning how to deal with clients on a daily basis. The manner in which such statistics are presented may be partly responsible for this problem. This sentiment is reflected in Hendin's (1982) comment that "social statistical profiles of the vulnerable have substituted for psychological understanding of suicide" (p. 17).

Caution is needed in applying statistics to suicide treatment and prevention. Using aggregate measures to predict individual behavior is fraught with dangers, especially when dealing with such a weighty concern as suicide. One cannot help but be concerned by the frequency with which one hears or reads the "modal profile" of the suicide victim (single or divorced white male, 45 years or older, etc.). It is not uncommon for inexperienced clinicians to judge a client's low risk because he or she does not "fit the profile."

In this chapter we seek to avoid the "numbers for numbers' sake" pitfall by primarily presenting statistics relevant to clinical questions. What behavioral and psychological characteristics can be regarded as warning signs for suicide potential? Can other characteristics serve as "buffers" against suicide risk? How do media representations of at-risk groups stack up against actual incidence figures? What can we learn from prevalence statistics to guide prevention efforts?

This chapter begins by examining the prevalence of phenomena much more common than suicide; that is, suicidal thinking and nonlethal suicidal behavior (parasuicide). Following this, we will present information on suicide fatalities from several standpoints, including international statistics, age and gender group comparisons, and risks posed by groups with various diagnostic and behavioral patterns. The last section describes possible "buffers" against suicide derived from epidemiological findings.

EPIDEMIOLOGY OF "BEING SUICIDAL"

Opinions vary on the accuracy of official estimates of the frequency of suicide. Writers commonly point out that suicide is grossly underestimated, some suggesting by as much as 100%. Reporting procedures vary considerably among states and cities, and deaths with "equivocal" causes (such as single-car accidents or fatal falls) range between 10% and 15%. Moreover, social, religious, and bureaucratic prejudices may bias the system in the direction of underreporting suicide. Coroners are thought sometimes to value the feelings of family members (not to mention financial concerns from insurance prohibitions against suicide) over whatever might be gained from more accurate reporting of suicide. However, an innovative study has recently challenged this conventional wisdom. By assuming that *all* accidental and undetermined deaths by causes commonly associated with suicide were indeed suicides, Kleck (1988) showed that the maximum amount by which suicides could possibly be underestimated is 46%; if drownings are eliminated, the figure drops to 22%. Thus, the axiom that suicide is grossly underestimated can no longer be simply assumed to be true.

Suicide and parasuicide almost of necessity begin with thoughts of suicide. Therefore, we will begin with an examination of the prevalence of suicidal thinking as a factor contributing to risk for eventual suicide or suicidal behavior.

Suicide Ideation

An interesting exercise in teaching classes and seminars about suicide is to ask participants to guess how common serious consideration of suicide is among the general population. Those who never have considered suicide even an option for themselves generally view suicidal thinking as aberrant and therefore a relatively rare phenomenon. Others, perhaps having experience with suicidality in themselves or significant others, predict thoughts of suicide to be more the rule than the exception. Empirical findings show this latter group to be closer to the truth.

Berman (1975) described several studies of the prevalence of suicidal thinking. Study samples ranged from college students to the general population, and none of these studies found suicidal ideation to be rare. The lowest prevalence estimate indicated that 40% of the population studied (college students) had given at least minimal consideration to suicide. Other estimates ranged from 50% to as high as 80% of nonclinical populations as having considered suicide at some point.

Shneidman (1971) conducted a survey through *Psychology Today* that drew over 30,000 responses. Over 50% of this sample acknowledged having seriously considered suicide at some time in their lives. More recently, Westefeld and Furr (1987) surveyed 962 students at three colleges/universities with differing demographic characteristics and found that from 24% to 46% acknowledged having thought about committing suicide. Linehan and Laffaw (1982) interviewed shoppers at a Seattle area mall and found that 24% reported a history of at least one episode of serious suicidal ideation. The authors point to the lack of anonymity as a possible reason why these figures are lower than findings of other studies. Regardless, suicidal thinking can hardly be considered a rare experience when it is reported by at least one in four persons in the general population. Any stigma or value judgments generally associated with suicide evidently have not led this substantial segment of the population to rule it out as a possible personal response to adversity.

It is probably reasonable to assume that the rate of suicidal thinking among psychotherapy clients will be higher. Obviously, rates can be expected to vary, depending on diagnostic classification, ranging from none to close to 100% in cases where being suicidal is among the diagnositic criteria (e.g., in the case of borderline personality disorder). In one study (Linehan & Laffaw, 1982), 31% of a general outpatient comparison group reported past or current suicidal thinking. Our experience in an acute care inpatient psychiatric setting has shown that two thirds of the patients admitted having suicidal ideation as part of their clinical presentation (unpublished data).

Parasuicide

The expression "parasuicide" was introduced by Kreitman (1977) as a term for all forms of intentional self-harming behavior. We will use it here to refer to acts labelled by the therapist or client as suicidal and not to "self-mutilation" (e.g., compulsively cutting or burning oneself without stated or apparent intent to commit suicide). Self-mutilation is seen in disorders as diverse as mental retardation and borderline personality disorder. While it may occur in persons with depression and suicidal tendencies, the self-mutilation syndrome appears to be functionally separate from suicidal behavior and may merit a separate diagnostic category (Pattison & Kahan, 1983).

The term parasuicide is preferable to such expressions as "suicide attempt" or "suicide gesture" because it implies neither motivation nor outcome. "Suicide attempt" suggests that an individual sought to end his or her life and somehow failed. In practice, therapists know that this is rarely the case. More commonly, various other motives come into play, and death is not the primary goal. Such expressions as "only a suicide gesture" or "nonserious attempt" carry perjorative overtones that imply that the individual is not "really" suicidal, but seeks to "manipulate" significant others.

While manipulative motives sometimes play a role, it stands to reason that any expression such as "nonserious suicide attempt" is a self-contradiction. Nonlethal suicidal behavior has highly disruptive effects on both the individual and his or her family. Often, the individual ends up in the hospital, with high costs both in terms of financial loss and the embarrassment and stigma of being a "psychiatric patient." Family members, perhaps already stressed from family conflicts, agonize over what role they might have played in this person's troubles and worry about an eventual fatal act. Service providers assume a share of the burden as well, wondering what they can do to prevent future, perhaps lethal, suicidal behavior.

Parasuicide is a major public health problem, occurring at least 10 times as often as suicide (Berman, 1975). Perhaps most important, as many as 15% of these individuals eventually do kill themselves (Murphy, 1985). Clearly, nonlethal suicidal behavior is not to be dismissed lightly. An expression such as parasuicide communicates the seriousness of the behavior while refraining from making inferences about motives or value judgments about the desirability of the act.

Parasuicide should be viewed separately from completed suicide because it involves a population with different characteristics from suicide completers (Murphy, 1985). Table 3.1 shows some of these differences. In contrast to suicide, which becomes more common among older populations and occurs two to three times more often among men, parasuicides occur predominantly among young persons and 1.5 to 3 times more often in females. Moreover, suicides generally use highly lethal, often violent methods for self-destruction, such as gunshot,

Table 3.1. Comparison of Suicide Attempters and Completers

Characteristic	Parasuicides	Suicides
Gender	Majority female	Majority male
Age	Predominantly young	Risk increases w/age
Method	Low lethality (pills, cutting)	More violent (gunshot, jumping)
Circumstances	Intervention likely	Precautions against discovery
Common diagnoses	Dysthymic disorder Borderline personality disorder	Major affective disorder Alcoholism Schizophrenia
Dominant affect	Depression with anger	Depression with hopelessness
Motivation	Change in situation Cry for help	Death
Hospital course	Quick recovery from dysphoria	Slow recovery with resistance or anger toward helpers
Attitude toward attempt	Relief to have survived Promises not to repeat	Regret to have survived

jumping, or hanging. Parasuicides, on the other hand, usually use methods of lower lethality (most often drug overdoses) and take few or no precautions against being discovered. Clinically, these individuals are usually observed to be relieved to be alive and to respond quickly to support, in contrast to failed suicides, who are often regretful to have survived and angry with those who intervened.

Differences between these two groups notwithstanding, it is essential to recognize a critical area of overlap between these two populations. It is estimated that 10% to 15% of parasuicides eventually will kill themselves. Moreover, 35% to 40% of people who commit suicide have made a previous attempt (Berman, 1975). Parasuicide remains the single best predictor of eventual suicide (Diekstra, 1973), a fact that must be taken into account when conducting clinical evaluations of suicide attempters.

As indicated above, parasuicide is far from uncommon. Berman (1975) describes several prevalence studies, placing the rate of U.S. parasuicides anywhere from 120 to 730 per 100,000 per year, compared with a rate of about 12 per 100,000 for suicide fatalities. He cites other studies showing that between 3.9% and 13% of the U.S. population has engaged in suicidal behavior on at least one occasion. Berman concludes from his review that over 10 million Americans had engaged in at least one moderately to seriously lethal suicide attempt. Given the increase in population and rates of parasuicide we can assume that this number is considerably higher now, over a decade later.

Table 3.2. Risk by Parasuicides for Future Attempts
and Completed Suicide

No further attempt	66%
Further attempts	33%
New attempt within 1 year	10%–20%
Completed suicide within 1 year	1%–2%
Completed suicide (lifetime)	10%–15%

In presenting data from Edinburgh, Kreitman (1981) reports highest rates of parasuicide among teenagers and young adults; the peak rate was among teenage girls, at about 1% per year. Ninety percent of parasuicides were by overdose, and about two thirds of males and almost as many females were drinking at the time. This study also showed dramatically higher rates of parasuicide among the lowest socioeconomic class. This finding has support in the United States as well (Linehan & Laffaw, 1982), although it is unclear whether this should be attributed to low income, stressful living conditions, unemployment, or some combination of variables.

Mental health professionals working with chronically suicidal people or repeat attempters may be surprised to learn that two thirds of attempters never make another attempt (Murphy, 1985). However, 10% to 20% will make a repeat attempt within a year; and about 10% will eventually take their lives, 1% to 2% within a year (Table 3.2).

SUICIDE COMPLETION

Frequency in Clinical Practice

Conventional clinical wisdom tells therapists, "It's not a matter of whether you'll have a client suicide but when." Empirical data on this topic are not abundant, but what is available suggests at least a kernel of truth in this observation. Of 131 psychiatrists responding to a recent national survey, 51% indicated that they had experienced a patient's suicide and half of these had experienced more than one (Chemtob, Hamada, Bauer, Kinney, & Torigoe, 1988). These figures compared with estimates ranging from 15% to 50% in earlier studies of psychiatrists or psychiatry residents. The authors concluded that patient suicide should be considered an "occupational hazard" for psychiatrists. Another study by the same authors showed that 22% of psychologists reported a patient's suicide and that the probability was related to years of training but not to years of clinical experience (Chemtob, et al., 1988). It is unknown at this point what might account for the lower rate among psy-

Table 3.3. Number and Rates of Suicide Deaths for Various U.S.
Populations (1970–1980)

Population	Deaths per year	Rate per 100,000
Overall	26,120	12.3
Males	19,012	18.0
White	17,610	18.9
African-Americans	1,402	11.3
Females	7,108	5.4
White	6,650	5.7
African-Americans	458	2.8
Age groups (yr)		
<15	142	.3
15–24	5,239	12.3
25–34	5,920	15.9
35–44	3,935	15.4
45–54	3,623	15.8
55–64	3,456	15.9
>65	4,537	18.2
Region		
Northeast	4,712	9.6
North Central	6,464	11.0
South	9,310	12.4
West	6,383	14.8

Note. From *Suicide surveillance report: United States, 1970–1980* by Centers for Disease
Control, 1985, Atlanta: U.S. Department of Health and Human Services.

chologists, although differing work settings and populations served must
be considered. At any rate, while the conventional wisdom stated above
may somewhat overstate the incidence of client suicide, it certainly can
be said that client suicide is far from unusual and should be considered
a possibility for every practicing clinician.

General Population

At least three people in the United States kill themselves every hour.
Suicide is the eighth or ninth leading cause of death, accounting for
about 1% of all deaths. The rate of U.S. suicides has remained fairly
constant over the past four decades at 11 to 12 per 100,000 per year.
This results in a conservative estimate of almost 30,000 deaths by suicide per year in the 1980s, about 10% greater than the annual number
of homicides (Holinger, 1987).

Suicide rates vary widely by age, gender, race, and geographic region. Table 3.3 shows rates and absolute numbers of suicides for these
variables according to the most recent 10-year report from the National
Centers for Disease Control (CDC, 1985). Clearly, white males constitute the highest risk group in the U.S. population. According to CDC
studies, fully 70% of suicides in the 1980s were committed by white

males. While this is partially attributable to their absolute numbers in the population, the suicide rate of 18.9 per 100,000 population shows that other factors (such as alcohol abuse and familiarity with firearms) come into play.

Also evident in Table 3.3, suicide risk as a general rule increases more-or-less linearly with age. Thus, the elderly continue to be the age group at highest risk for suicide. White men over 50 make up only 10% of the population but account for 28% of suicides. While youth suicide has grown alarmingly since the 1950s—by as much as 300 percent— these rates have increased only to the overall population mean of about 12 per 100,000. On the other hand, persons over age 60 make up 40% of suicides but only 20% of the general population.

Important exceptions exist to the general rule of higher risk among persons who are older and white. For example, statistics showing positive correlation between age and suicide rates may be reflecting mainly the predominance of suicides among white males. Holinger (1987) reports that peak suicide rates occur in the 35 to 64 age range among white females and in the 25 to 34 age range among nonwhite males and females. Other research suggests that studies showing correlations between age and suicide rates may largely be reflecting the higher prevalence of widowhood and divorce among older persons. In analyzing data collected in Scotland, Kreitman (1988) showed that marital status correlates more highly with suicide rates than age and that adjusting for marital status produces reductions in elderly suicide rates and increases in youth rates. In fact, the highest rate in this study occurred among young widowed persons.

Nor is the relationship between race and suicide without qualification. As a rule, studies show that suicide rates among whites are significantly greater than rates among nonwhites (CDC, 1985). However, in urban settings the suicide rate among young African-American males is double the rate for young white males (Hendin, 1982). Comparisons between whites and Native-Americans are also complex and hinge on the particular tribe in question. While rates among some tribes are below the national average, rates have been found to be alarmingly high in the Southwest Pueblos (27.8 per 100,000) and Apaches (43.3 per 100,000) (Berlin, 1987). Suicide rates among Hispanics appear to be uniformly lower than among whites, though suicide is by no means uncommon (Sorenson & Golding, 1988).

Geographic Factors

International figures generally show the suicide rate in the United States (12 per 100,000 per year) to be about average for an industrialized nation. The highest rates occur in eastern Europe (topped by Hungary), German-speaking countries, Scandinavia, and Japan (generally over 25 per 100,000). Lowest rates are reported by Greece, Ireland, and Italy (all below 6 per 100,000) (Shneidman, 1976; Kreitman, 1981).

Suicide rates in the United States also vary considerably by region. As shown in Table 3.3, suicide rates are lowest in the northeast, with New Jersey having the lowest rate in the United States at 7.4 per 100,000. The highest suicide rates occur in the west; Nevada has the highest suicide rate in the country at 22.9 per 100,000. Rates in the west decreased in the last decade and increased slightly in the rest of the country (CDC, 1985).

Incidence of suicide also is associated with urbanization. Generally speaking, suicide rates increase more-or-less with the size of cities. A rural exception to this rule might be communities where agriculture is in decline and migration to cities is occurring (Sainsbury, 1986).

Trends

Recent trends in suicide rates have been dominated by the rise in suicides among young persons, particularly males. As stated earlier, the suicide rate for young adults has tripled during the past 25 years. White males ages 15 to 39 represented less than one fourth of suicides (23%) in the 1960s and over one third (35%) in the 1970s. While the acceleration in youth suicide seemed to have begun to decline after peaking in 1977, recent analyses have shown that this is true only for the upper end of the 15 to 24 age group; the rate for persons ages 15 to 19 reached another record high in 1985 (Fingerhut & Kleinman, 1988).

In the United States, the gap between the sexes remains significant and in fact appears to be widening. While the incidence of suicide among white and nonwhite men remained relatively constant between 1950 and 1983, rates for white women dropped from 7.2 (per 100,000) in 1970 to 5.6 in 1983. The suicide rate for black females fell from 3.5 in 1975 to 2.6 in 1983 (Suicide: An Update, 1986).

While elderly people continue to exhibit the highest rate of suicide, the rate among the elderly recently has declined somewhat. During the period following 1950, over two thirds of all suicides were committed by people age 45 and older; but by 1980, the majority had shifted, the elderly accounting for only two fifths of suicides, and the 15 to 44 age group accounting for three fifths of suicides (Suicide: An Update, 1986). In fact, the occurrence of suicide has increased so much among young African-Americans that their rate has surpassed the rate among older African-Americans (Berman, 1975). This has coincided with increasing violence and homicide among urban African-Americans. Among all

Table 3.4. Estimated Suicide Rates for Major Psychiatric
Diagnoses (ranges shown where estimates differ)

Diagnosis	Annual Rate per 100,000
Depression	230–566
Schizophrenia	167–750
Alcoholism	133–270
Personality disorder	130
Neurosis	119
Organic brain disorder	78

Sources: Pokorny (1974), Sainsbury (1986), Roy (1986), Suicide Research Digest (April, 1988).

populations, firearms are accounting for an increasing proportion of suicides (CDC, 1985).

Risk Factors

In addition to population surveys, clinical studies also have assessed relative suicide risk for subpopulations. Most notable among these are studies of various diagnostic groups. Studies have shown that the vast majority of persons committing suicide were suffering from one or more psychiatric disturbances at the time; probably less than 1% were suffering from no diagnosable psychiatric disorder (Klerman, 1987). As many as 80% were suffering from some form of depression, 20% to 30% from alcoholism, up to 12% from schizophrenia, and perhaps 10% percent from organic brain syndrome (Murphy, 1985); approximately one in five was probably psychotic at the time of death (Robins, 1986).

Clinicians are sometimes surprised to learn how common suicide is among people with various psychiatric disorders. As many as 30% of people suffering from major affective disorders die by suicide (Klerman, 1987), an alarmingly high mortality rate for any illness. Two other psychiatric disorders pose high risk for eventual suicide. Estimates of lifetime risk for suicide among alcoholics range from 15% to 25%; the rate for schizophrenics is 10% to 20% (Klerman, 1987). Finally, Seager (1986) estimates that 25% of suicides are committed by persons with neurotic and personality disorders. Table 3.4 shows estimates of suicide rates per 100,000 for some diagnostic groups. Clearly, accurate diagnosis carries important implications regarding treatment planning and precautions against suicide.

The relationship between suicide and physical illness is less clear and probably varies with the particular illness and population in question (Suicide Research Digest, 1988). Estimates of the prevalence of physical illness in completed suicide range from 25% to 70%, with illness as a contributing cause to the suicide in 11% to 51% (Whitlock, 1986). Loss of functional ability appears to elevate suicide risk, especially among the elderly; one study showed that one half of elderly males had been suffering from some chronic illness such as cancer or cardiovascular disease before committing suicide (Gatter & Bowen, 1980). AIDS victims may also be at particular risk: One study has placed the rate of suicide among AIDS patients at no less than 345 per 100,000 (Marzuk et al., 1988). These rates are comparable with those in the major psychiatric disorders (see Table 3.4).

At least one study runs counter to the general finding of elevated risk associated with various diseases. Brown et al. (1986) showed that from 44 patients with terminal cancer, only 3 had considered suicide and that all of these were clinically depressed. More research obviously is needed to clarify this relationship, but it is evident that what is labelled as "rational suicide" in cases of terminal illness may often be precipitated by a depressive disorder and therefore unlikely to be truly rational.

Incarcerated adults form a special, high-risk population for suicide. In the most recently available data from the Bureau of Justice Statistics, 294 people killed themselves while in local jails during the 12-month period preceding June 30, 1983, when the national jail census was 223,551. This represents a suicide rate of 132 per 100,000 jail inmates, a rate *ten times the national average*. (This rate is probably an overestimate, since the jail census for one day does not represent the total number of people jailed and released during the year when the 294 suicides occurred.) In contrast, the suicide rate in prison, where convicted felons serve sentences longer than one year, is no higher than the national average (10 to 14 per 100,000). Whatever the "true" suicide rated for incarcerated adults, a high-risk population is formed by the typical jail suicide profile: a 22-year-old, single, white male who has been arrested for an alcohol-related offense and who attempts suicide within 24 hours of arrest (Hess, 1987).

Social Factors and Suicide

Sociological studies show that suicide rates also are associated with historical and economic events. For example, Holinger (1987) presented data showing clear peaks during the early 1900s and the Great Depression and valleys during the two World Wars. In his analysis of the relationship between economic conditions and mental illness, Brenner (1973) showed a strong association between suicide rates and such economic indicators as inflation and unemployment. More recently, Sainsbury (1986) described multivariate studies of social trends in several

European countries associating increases in the suicide rate with indicators of decreased family cohesion, changes in women's status (e.g., increases in female employment and teenage pregnancy), and increasing general affluence. Commenting on the ability of such social variables to predict rises and falls in suicide rates, the author highlights two points: "The extent to which changing social conditions affect national trends in suicide and the consistency with which certain socioeconomic developments, notably unemployment and women's roles in society, contribute to its incidence" (pp. 34–35).

The relationship between socioeconomic status and suicide is complex. Some studies have indicated that higher risk is associated with higher income, education, and occupational status, while other data suggest higher risk at both ends of the economic spectrum. Moreover, dynamic factors also play a role. For example, there is some indication that while long-term poverty does not increase risk, downward mobility (loss of social status) probably does (Sainsbury, 1986). In addition, unemployment has reliably been associated with increased suicide risk (Platts, 1984), although it is unclear whether unemployment increases suicide risk or existing psychopathology increases risk of both unemployment and suicide. At present, a reasonable point of view is expressed by Sainsbury (1986): "The probability is that it is a nexus of such considerations which is responsible: an interaction of socioeconomic circumstances, psychological vulnerability, and stressful events" (p. 27).

Considerable evidence exists for an absence of social support in the lives of suicidal persons (Linehan, 1981). Both suicidal and parasuicidal persons are more often unemployed or retired than nonsuicidal persons and therefore without the support provided by an employment setting. It is also evident from clinical experience that suicidal persons very often come from nonsupportive or hostile family environments.

Marital status may be the aspect of social support with the greatest influence on suicide risk. Nonmarried status represents a risk factor in people who are (in order of decreasing levels of risk) separated, divorced, widowed, or single (Sainsbury, 1986). People who have never been married are twice as likely to suicide as married people, and divorced and widowed persons have even higher rates (Suicide: Part 1, 1986). Several studies have shown that absence of a spouse, whether due to death, separation, or divorce, increases the probability of suicidal behavior, although these data are not without their ambiguities (Linehan, 1981). As mentioned earlier, Kreitman (1988) showed marital status to be even more strongly correlated with suicide risk than age.

The relationship of religion to suicide remains somewhat unclear. Durkheim's early research indicated that, perhaps due to doctrinal pro-

hibitions against suicide, Catholics had lower suicide rates than Prot-
estants; but more recent studies have failed to confirm this finding.
Religious *involvement* might be a better predictor than church doctrines.
Maris (1981) found that people who had committed suicide had partic-
ipated less in religious activities than a comparison group. Martin (1984)
showed that the rank ordering of gender and race groups according to
suicide rates duplicated the order of church attendance in reverse (i.e.,
white males attended church the least and African-American females
attended the most).

SUMMARY

Epidemiological studies show that parasuicide is a major clinical and
public health problem, epidemiologically (and clinically) distinct from
completed suicide. It occurs at a rate many times higher than that of
suicide and remains the best single predictor of eventual suicide. Populations at highest risk for parasuicide are adolescents and young adults,
particularly females. Also included among major risk factors are alcohol consumption, divorce, and low socioeconomic status.

While relationships are complex, risk of completed suicide can generally be assumed to be higher in groups who are older, male, white,
unemployed; have higher incidence of psychiatric disorders such as
depression and alcoholism; and lack social supports such as marriage
and church involvement. Exceptions to the general race and age guidelines are young, African-American males in urban settings and certain
tribes of Native-Americans. Women are at greatest risk in the 35 to 64
age range for whites and the 25 to 34 age range for nonwhites.

Conversely, certain factors might be regarded as "buffers" against
suicide, and consequently might be considered as areas for therapeutic
intervention. These include social support, particularly in the form of
a stable and supportive family, stable employment, church involvement, and lower levels of depression and substance abuse. Suicide
buffers will be discussed further in Chapter 9.

Chapter 4
Decision Making for Suicide Risk

The assessment of a client's potential suicide risk requires the gathering and weighing of a variety of information and data. While all assessments and therapy require ongoing decision making, the importance of a thorough and comprehensive suicidal assessment has led to our development of a decision model that integrates and formalizes the steps for a thorough and reasonable judgment about the risk for suicide by an individual client. Figure 4.1 presents the suggested flowchart for the assessment of suicidal risk. Similar to the decision models in the *Diagnostic and Statistical Manual of Mental Disorders (DSM-III-R)* (1987) to assist diagnostic choices, this table outlines specific steps for data collection, choice points, and a path of subsequent actions depending on the prior decision. There are seven sequentially numbered steps for a therapist. This chapter will discuss steps 1 through 4: (1) demographic information, (2) clinical indicators, (3) initial screening, and (4) direct assessment of suicide risk.

DEMOGRAPHIC INFORMATION

Step 1 (of Figure 4.1) involves the gathering of demographic information about your client. The age, sex, race, marital status, and living situation are all relevant factors that should be considered to determine whether your client is in a high- or low-risk group of the population at large. Table 4.1 is a demographic screening checklist that summarizes the major variables to be considered. Each demographic factor will be discussed below. Chapter 3 provided a detailed review of the research that supports these guidelines.

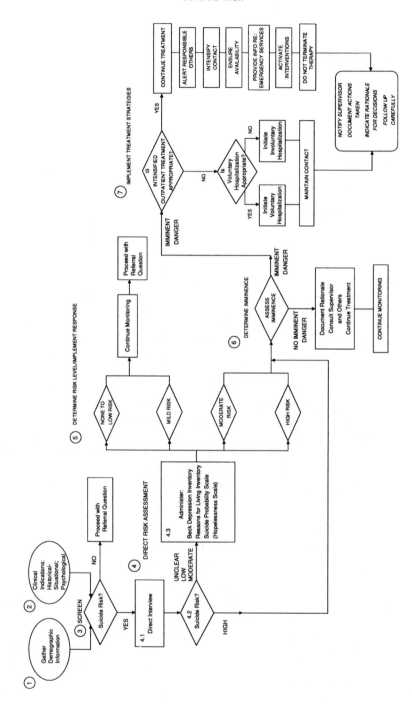

Table 4.1. Demographic Suicide Risk Indicators

	Risk Level	
	Low	High
Sex		
Male		————
Female	————	
Age (yr)		
White males		
0–45	————	
45+		————
White females		
0–34, 66+	————	
35–65		————
Nonwhites, male/female		
0–24, 35+	————	
25–34		————
Race		
White		————
Nonwhite	————	
Marital status		
Married	————	
Single, divorced, widowed		————
Living arrangements		
Family and friends	————	
Solitary		————
Environment		
Rural	————	
Urban		————
Employment		
Employed	————	
Unemployed		————

Sex

Males of all ages are a greater suicide risk than females. Males complete suicide three times more often than women, although women have three times more parasuicides than men. Females aged 15 to 35 are most likely to have parasuicidal behaviors (Centers for Disease Control, 1985) than other age groups.

Age

In general, as age increases the risk of suicide potential increases. For white males, the risk of suicide increases as age increases. White females, however, are at greatest risk between the ages of 33 and 64 years and then the risk decreases. Among nonwhite males and females, the 25 to 34 year period is the greatest risk period (Centers for Disease Control, 1985).

Race

Recorded suicide rates in the United States are higher for whites than for nonwhites. White males account for approximately 70% of the total completed suicides (Centers for Disease Control, 1985). Overall, the suicide rates among nonwhites are traditionally about one half the rate of that of whites. However, suicide rates among some tribes of Native-Americans, such as the Apaches, are much higher than the general population (Berlin, 1987).

Marital Status

Divorced, widowed, or separated individuals have higher suicide risks than those who are married (Sainsbury, 1986).

Living Arrangements

Solitary living arrangements heighten suicide risk compared with living with family or close friends (Linehan, 1981).

Environment

People who live in urban environments are at a higher risk for suicide than people in suburban or rural environments (Sainsbury, 1986).

Employment

People who are unemployed are at a higher risk than people who have steady employment (Platts, 1984).

Discussion

Overall, demographic variables are useful to identify groups of individuals who may be at risk for suicidal behavior. However, demographic variables have very little practical utility in the assessment of a specific individual. The sex and race of an individual do not change across his or her life. This information does not provide data necessary for the assessment of the current risk that an individual may be experiencing. These factors are complex and often form specific interactions of several variables to create the highest risk groups. Therefore, the simple demographic factors are offered as a very basic set of information to alert the therapist that a client may be a member of a high risk group. Demographic factors must not be the sole criteria for the assessment of risk. These factors should only be considered in addition to the following clinical indicators.

Table 4.2. Historical-Situational Suicide Risk Factors

	Low	Moderate	High
1. Daily functioning	Fairly good in most activities	Moderately good	Impaired in activities
2. Life-style	Stable	Some changes	Unstable
3. Coping style and resources	Adequate resources Constructive coping	Some resources Some coping	Inadequate resources Destructive coping
4. Significant others	Multiple people available	Few available	One or more available
5. Psychiatric history	None or good response to prior treatment	Prior treatment	Uncooperative in prior treatment
6. Medical history	Healthy	Mild problems	Chronic illnesses
7. Family history of suicide	None	Parasuicide acts	Suicides within family
8. Previous suicidal acts	None	One to multiple attempts Mild to moderate lethality	Multiple attempts of high lethality

CLINICAL INDICATORS

In the decision making chart, step 2, historical and clinical indicators are the individual characteristics of the client that more specifically heighten or lower a client's risk for suicide. These are the unique historical, environmental, and current psychological features that the client presents at intake or during therapy. The therapist, during an intake and over subsequent sessions, should gather the information that is summarized in Tables 4.2 and 4.3. This information is organized from general historical factors, which begin to raise suicide risk, to very specific clinical indicators and warning signs that may precede imminent attempts, such as making a suicide plan or having final arrangements made for a will and burial. Based on the factors proposed by Hatton, Valente, and Rink (1977), Table 4.2 summarizes the historical and environmental factors that should be gathered. Table 4.3 presents the current psychological indicators to assess the risk of a particular client in addition to the demographic risk factors.

Historical-Situational Indicators

Daily functioning. An individual with adequate daily functioning in most activities, such as being able to maintain a household, socialize, and function adequately at work, is at low risk. A high-risk person has poor social functioning in these major areas. This is similar to the Global Assessment of Functioning (GAF) Scale of the DSM-III-R. An individ-

Table 4.3. Short-Term Clinical Suicide Risk Factors

	Low	Moderate	High
1. Recent losses	None	Within last month	Within days of loss
2. Depression-anxiety	Mild	Moderate	Severe
3. Isolation-withdrawal	Regular social contacts	Some social contact	Socially isolated
4. Hostility	Mild	Moderate	Severe
5. Hopelessness	Mild	Moderate	Severe
6. Disorientation-disorganization	None	Moderate	Severe
7. Alcohol/drug abuse	None to little	Frequent to excess	Chronic abuse
8. Change in clinical features	None		Unexplained improvement
9. Suicidal plan[a]			
9.1 Method	Undecided	Decided	Decided
9.2 Availability	No	Yes	Yes
9.3 Time-place	Not specific	Not specific	Yes
9.4 Lethality	Low	Moderate	High
10. Final arrangements	None	Some planning	Written note, wills, possessions given away

[a]Determined from direct interview about suicidal thoughts and plan.

ual with a high GAF Scale rating is at lower risk than a person with a lower GAF Scale rating.

Life-style. A stable life-style in terms of a stable living situation, friends, and a job suggest a lower risk for suicide than a person who has had frequent changes or disruptions in these important areas. A stable life-style provides a psychological foundation from which a person may be better able to cope with a psychological crisis that could lead to suicidal thoughts or actions.

Coping ability. A person who has coped with prior life changes and crises constructively is at a lower risk than a person who previously displayed destructive acts or inadequate coping strategies when in crises. For example, a person who has abused alcohol and/or drugs, has run away, has been violent toward others, or has displayed suicidal behaviors has a history of poor coping strategies to prior life situations. The presence of these prior problems heightens the risk for future inadequate coping with current situations. Conversely, a person who has coped with crises in the past through effective problem-solving, use of family and social resources, or use of appropriate professional help has shown higher levels of past coping skills. This suggests that the person would be better equipped to deal adequately with a current crisis without suicidal acts.

Significant others. The presence of several significant others in a person's immediate life lessens the risk of suicide. These people may provide support, resources, and potential help to effectively cope with a current crisis. A person without significant others may feel socially isolated and alone in coping with current problems. This feeling of social isolation and loneliness is a significant factor in increasing the risk of suicide.

Psychiatric history. An individual with no history of prior psychiatric disorder or treatment is at lower risk than a person who has had prior major psychiatric problems. In particular, a diagnosis of schizophrenia, affective disorder, alcoholism, or a personality disorder indicates a higher risk for life-threatening behaviors (Klerman, 1987).

Medical history. A person who is physically healthy has a lower risk for suicide than a person who is attempting to cope with chronic or terminal physical illness. Patients diagnosed with AIDS or who are HIV positive are at extremely high risk (Marzuk et al., 1988). The therapist should assess the individual's current health, particularly recent surgeries, illnesses, or physiological changes that may indicate declining health and physical problems. The date of the client's last physical exam should be obtained. Assess the current medications to alert the therapist to the presence of significant physical problems. In addition, the presence of these medications may heighten the risk of suicidal acts by providing a convenient means for a lethal suicide attempt.

Family history of suicide. Individuals with no family history of suicide by immediate family or relatives are at lower risk than a person from a family in which significant others committed suicide. In this latter group, suicide has been modeled within the family and increases the probability of a family member attempting or completing suicide.

Previous suicide attempts. A person with no prior suicide attempts is at lower risk than a person who has had multiple attempts of self-destruction. As summarized in Table 3.2, if a person has attempted suicide at least once, the lifetime risk of dying by suicide is 10% to 15% (Murphy, 1985). The history of an individual's prior suicide attempts is the most significant historical factor that must be considered in assessing current suicide risk.

Berman (1975) reported that 35% to 40% of actual suicide victims had made prior unsuccessful attempts. One to two percent of suicide attempters kill themselves within 1 year of the first attempt. Individuals who attempt a suicide are more likely to attempt it again. Those who have made prior attempts are more than likely to be successful with an attempt than people with no prior suicidal experience. Second attempts are likely to occur within 3 months of the first attempt.

Discussion. The previously discussed historical and situational or environmental factors provide additional information about the individual's risk factors. Table 4.3 summarizes the more immediate psychological factors that must be considered when assessing the immediate risk of suicide. These factors are discussed in order from general to very specific risk factors of increasing importance.

Psychological Indicators

Recent losses. A person with few or no recent losses in his or her life is at a lower risk for suicide than a person who has just realized a major loss, such as the death of a spouse, divorce, death of a child, or loss of a job. The more life changes the person has experienced, the higher risk for physical and psychological distress. Recent losses are environmental events but they may create an immediate crisis that challenges the person's ability to cope.

Depression-Anxiety. The client who is not experiencing high levels of depression or anxiety is at lower risk than a client who has high levels of subjective distress, depression, or anxiety. This high level of distress may be a motivating factor to lead a person to consider and attempt suicide to end the unhappiness. Eighty percent of the people who commit suicide are depressed at the time of their act (Murphy, 1985).

Isolation-Withdrawal. An individual who continues to have regular social contacts and to be integrated within a social network is at lower risk than a person who has become socially isolated. Similar to a person who does not have significant others, the socially isolated or withdrawn person is at heightened risk to commit suicide because he or she does not have others to help with psychological support and problem-solving, or to provide resources to help deal with the immediate crisis. The person may have significant others but may have withdrawn from them. This is a sign of heightened risk if the person is isolating him or herself from these other resources. Therefore, either the socially isolated person or the person who has become withdrawn and isolated is at a higher risk than a person who continues to interact regularly and meaningfully with others.

Hostility. A person without a history of hostility toward him or herself or others is at a lower risk than a person who has a prior history of anger and hostility expressed toward others. Anger and hostility are prominent dimensions in the assessment of immediate suicidal risk (Cull & Gill, 1982).

Hopelessness. A person who does not feel hopeless about the future is at lower risk for suicide than a person who sees no hope for the future. Hopelessness is not synonymous with depression and is a separate dimension. Hopelessness is a pessimistic perception of the future and the negative view that events will change for the better. Hopelessness is a significantly high risk psychological factor for suicidal acts (Bedrosian & Beck, 1979; Beck, Brown, & Steer, 1989).

Disorientation-Disorganization. A person who is in touch with reality and shows no impairment of his or her thinking processes is at lower risk than a person who has had problems maintaining contact with reality and thinking rationally. Among people who experience psychotic episodes, command hallucinations may be the antecedent for an impulsive suicidal or homicidal act. Command hallucinations are auditory hallucinations in which a voice orders or directs the person to carry out specific behaviors. The presence of disorganized thinking may heighten the risk of the suicidal act because of the person's inability to rationally control and evaluate his or her actions. Persons with either schizophrenia or organic brain syndrome may experience these problems of disorientation or irrational thinking, which can contribute to their higher rate of suicide.

Alcohol and drug abuse. A person who does not abuse alcohol is at lower risk than a person who has a history of chronic substance abuse. Alcohol and drugs lower the emotional and behavioral controls that may prevent a person from attempting suicide. In addition, substance abuse may also be associated with loss of family support, unemployment, social isolation, and other risk-heightening factors. Robins (1985) reported that alcoholism, along with depression, are the two psychiatric illnesses predominantly associated with completed suicides. Both alcoholism and depression are present in approximately 70% of the completed suicides that he studied.

Change in clinical features. A client who presents with a consistent clinical picture of depression, anxiety, or hostility is at less immediate risk for a suicidal act than a person who makes a sudden and unexplained change in his or her clinical and psychological functioning. There is often a spontaneous improvement in affect that cannot be explained by treatment or therapeutic interventions. This positive change is often later explained as the tranquility associated with the patient's decision to end his or her life by suicide. This decision resolves the ambivalence and distress that may have been observed as depression and anxiety.

The highest risk of suicide exists toward the end of a depressive episode and not at the most severe level of a depressive episode (Kreitman, 1986). Therefore, if a client suddenly appears improved in the absence of any clear reason for this improvement, he or she may have made a decision to commit suicide and needs to be thoroughly evaluated for immediate suicide risk.

Suicide plan. Suicide plans can be assessed in terms of the method, the availability of the method, the specific knowledge about how to implement the plan in terms of time and place, and the overall lethality of the plan. The person with an undecided means to kill him or herself and without specific time or place to do this is at lower risk than a person who has decided on a lethal means of death (such as a gunshot), has the method available, and has selected a time and place for this attempt. The more specific, available, and deadly the plan, the higher the possibility that the person will implement the plan.

Final arrangements. If a person has not made any final plans for his or her death, such as writing a suicide note, giving away possessions, or making final arrangements for care of pets and children, then the risk is lower than someone who has taken steps to complete these final arrangements for death. The presence of a suicide note, a recently changed will, or the giving away of prized personal possessions are all very high risk indicators of an imminent attempt.

Discussion The above tables provide 18 factors or symptoms that should be considered in evaluating a client's current suicide risk. There is no simple formula to add or combine these factors. The clinician's experience and judgment must be used. The presence of even one high-risk factor, such as a suicide note, may be enough to indicate that there is high risk for suicide. In contrast, the presence of four or five risk factors, such as unstable life-style and few significant others, may not signal imminent risk. The factors are presented in increasing order of importance for an imminent suicide attempt. As high-risk factors emerge toward the end of the list, the clinician should be increasingly aware of the potential suicide risk of the client.

Following the accumulation of the information outlined previously, a client's unique emotional and psychological state should be considered in total. Motto (1977) said,

> in any given patient, however, the numerous predictive variables collated with subsequent suicide give us only limited assistance. The common denominator of all the factors conducive to suicide is psychic pain and since every person experiences a given situation in a unique way, it

is necessary to first determine the level of pain created by the patient's situation and second to ascertain how close that level is to the person's limit of tolerance. Those with a low threshold may thus be highly suicidal with only moderate stress, while others are not at risk in spite of severe stress. This largely accounts to the absence of any generally accepted predictive scale, psychological test or other measuring device of suicidal risk. (p. 2)

INITIAL SCREENING

Based on information about the client's demographic characteristics (step 1), combined with knowledge of the client's historical and psychological characteristics (step 2), the therapist should make an informed decision as to whether there is potential suicide risk that warrants further assessment. If the demographic characteristics and clinical indicators are both negative, then assessment and treatment can progress along other areas of assessment. If, however, there are risk factors indicated by either the demographic profile, or more specifically, by historical and clinical symptoms, then the clinician should directly assess current risk for suicide through an interview.

DIRECT ASSESSMENT

Direct Interview

It is essential that a clinician faced with a potentially suicidal client directly address this issue. Discussing the possibility of self-destructive behavior does not increase the likelihood that the client will complete the act. On the contrary, the client may feel relieved in finding someone with whom to share extremely personal and distressing thoughts. In addition, the client's feelings of isolation and hopelessness may be reduced by such a candid discussion.

The therapist should approach these sensitive issues in a nonthreatening, empathetic, and nonjudgmental manner. It is important that the questions be asked in a calm and quiet way while the therapist refrains from expressing shock, disbelief, or moral judgments. The issues and parameters that should be examined in the interview are outlined in the following list. It is not always necessary to ask every question, but these are offered to give a suggested progression of questions to assess the current thoughts and plans for suicide. Questions start out generally and progress to very specific inquiries. Note that the questions use the term suicide directly and do not use euphemisms such as "ending it all, going to heaven, meeting your maker," and so forth. Suicide should not be portrayed in a poetic or metaphorical way.

Direct Interview Sample Questions

1. Have you ever felt depressed for several days at a time?
2. During this time, have you ever had thoughts of killing yourself?
3. When did these thoughts occur?
4. What did you think about doing to yourself?
5. Did you act on your thoughts?
6. How often have these thoughts occurred?
7. When is the last time you had these thoughts?
8. Have your thoughts ever included harming someone else in addition to yourself?
9. How often has that occurred?
10. What have you thought about doing to the other person?
11. What would the outcome or benefit be of this act toward this other person?
12. When does this thought occur?
13. Recently, what specifically have you thought about doing to yourself?
14. Have you taken any steps towards acquiring the "gun, pills," and so forth?
15. Have you thought about when you would do this?
16. Have you thought about where you would do this?
17. Have you thought about what effect your death would have on your family?
18. Have you thought about what effect your death would have on your friends and others?
19. You sound ambivalent or unsure about these plans. What are some of the reasons that have kept you from acting on them thus far?
20. More specifically, what are your feelings about religion, suicide, and God?
21. What are your thoughts about your responsibilities for your family and children if you kill yourself?
22. What are your thoughts about other reasons for living and staying alive?
23. What help could make it easier for you to cope with your current thoughts and plans?
24. Have you made any plans for your possessions or to communicate with people after your death such as a note or a will?
25. How does talking about this made you feel?

The following is a sample interview between a therapist and an outpatient client, Mr. Lane, in which the therapist is directly assessing the client's suicide risk. In this example, the client is being seen for an intake session at a community mental health center. The following information was collected by the intake worker before the client was seen by the therapist.

The client is a 27-year-old white, divorced man who has no prior history of inpatient or outpatient psychiatric care. He had been employed as a coal miner until he injured his back two years ago. He has had a variety of medical and physical therapy treatments with little reported benefit. He has been unable to return to work and is now reporting an increase in feelings of depression and pain. He takes 10 to 12 aspirin each day for pain.

The client has been living with his parents since his divorce. He has a three-year-old son and a five-year-old daughter who live with his ex-wife and he sees them two weekends each month. The client reports to be episodically drinking alcohol, primarily beer, to the point of intoxication. He denies other drug use. He has no history of legal difficulties. The patient completed high school with average grades and began working one year later as a miner. He worked steadily until suffering this back injury.

A brief mental status exam showed that he was oriented and knew the time, person, and place; had adequate short-term concentration of six digits forward and four backwards; could deal with some proverbs in a concrete manner such as "a stitch in time means if you sew up your pants now they won't rip." The client denies any current or previous delusions, auditory visual hallucinations, thought insertion, thought broadcasting, or ideas of reference.

A review of biological symptoms reveals a poor appetite and a 25-lb weight loss during the last year. The patient complains of sleep onset disturbance, frequent awakenings, and feelings of fatigue upon awakening. His sexual drive is reduced from before his injury and he has occasional headaches.

Subjectively the client says, "All this pain and depression is getting too much for me. I am just getting tired of this." He presented with serious affect but could smile occasionally. Generally, he avoided eye contact.

Plan: Refer Mr. Lane for further evaluation and therapy by a primary therapist. There is a serious question about the severity of depression and potential suicide risk based on his demographic profile, presence of depression, and feelings of distress.

Sample Interview

Therapist: What has your mood been like recently?
Patient: Lousy. I am just sick of hurting.
Therapist: Have you been depressed?
Patient: What do you think? I hurt all the time. The medicine doesn't help, the therapy doesn't help. I can't do what I used to do. Yeah, I'm depressed.
Therapist: Sounds like it has been real rough for you.
Patient: Yeah. I have always been able to handle other things. I have always been strong and I could fight and win. This pain just doesn't end.

Therapist: Do you get to the point where you sometimes feel like crying?

Patient: I feel like crying but I don't let myself in front of people. Sometimes I would rather scream. I can't stand it. There is nothing I can do to get comfortable. The doctors say I just have to learn to live with it. I would like to see them learn to live with it.

Therapist: What do you think your future would be like in a year?

Patient: I don't have any future. I just try to not think about it. My future was shot when that rock fell on me. It is all shot.

Therapist: Have you had thoughts of killing yourself?

Patient: Wouldn't you?

Therapist: I can understand how you may have had these thoughts with all the pain you have experienced.

Patient: Yeah, I have thought about it. I am thinking about it more recently.

Therapist: What have you thought about doing to kill yourself?

Patient: The new dam is near my house. I have been up there looking down over the edge. I thought about just jumping off and ending the pain.

Therapist: When were you last up there?

Patient: About 3 weeks ago I went up there. I was having a day where I just couldn't take it. I had some beer on the way over there. I was going to do it. It was going to be the end of this. My kids don't need me anymore. I can't work. I can't provide for them. I couldn't even kill myself. I'm a failure at that. I chickened out.

Therapist: Some people would say that jumping is the chicken way out. How close did you come to killing yourself?

Patient: I got there, I took out my wallet and looked at a picture of my kids to say goodbye to them. Then I thought I couldn't do it to them. I may not be much of a Dad to them but I'm their only Dad. I don't want someone else marrying their Mom and them never knowing me. So I got back in the car and went home.

Therapist: I'm glad you did and were able to come in and ask for some help. Have you had the thoughts recently of harming yourself?

Patient: No, since I made this appointment I figure I could give you a chance to help me. Although I know nothing can really help.

Therapist: Your children sound like an important reason for you to stay alive. Tell me more about them.

Patient: They are real special kids. They are the best part of my life. Everybody says Joey looks just like me and Mary looks like her Mom. I just can't see them enough. When I started thinking about hurting them that is what made me stop. I got to stay around to help them grow up.

Therapist: Those are two wonderful reasons to keep trying. Other than jumping off the bridge, have you ever had any other thoughts about how to kill yourself?

Patient: I guess I could crash my car into something but I have never really thought about it. We don't have any guns in the house. No, just jumping was all I have ever really considered.

Therapist: How much control do you feel you have right now about your thoughts of killing yourself?

Patient: Today is not too bad. It kinda helps to talk about it. I was thinking I was going crazy but sometimes this pain just doesn't quit. No one seems to understand. Today it is better.

Therapist: What kind of help do you think you need?

Patient: I need to talk to someone. It just gets all bottled up inside. I'm by myself too much. I guess I need to get busy.

Therapist: Do you feel that you need to be in a safe place right now such as a hospital?

Patient: No, no. I'm not crazy. I'm okay. I don't need to be in a hospital. Coming here and talking is helping.

Therapist: At this point in your life, how much do you want to live versus how much do you want to die? Can you give me a percentage about how much you want to live?

Patient: Today I want to live 81%. How's that, doc? I think the day I was on the dam it was 50–50. Today is better.

Therapist: Okay. Let's start talking about today and tomorrow and making some plans to make it better. Periodically I am going to ask you about whether you are having any thoughts of killing yourself. I want you to be honest with me. Do you promise me?

Patient: Yeah, I promise. But like I said, I am not nuts or crazy but this pain is just hard to live with sometimes.

Therapist: It sure sounds like it has been a rough struggle for you.

The above sample interview shows a frustrated, somewhat hostile client who quickly reveals suicidal thoughts and a prior near lethal plan. The interviewer attempted to assess the presence of current thoughts and plans as distinguished from previous ones. The interviewer also solicited the client's reasons for living and tried to reinforce those important motivations to work to improve. The client's two young children and a competitive feeling of not wanting his ex-wife's new husband to raise his children were identified as motivating factors to keep him alive and coping with his own physical and psychological problems. The interviewer attempted to offer hope for the future by offering to work toward specific plans to improve the client's life. The interviewer also offered hope by offering admission to an inpatient unit. This revealed caring and showed the client that there were options in a place where he could receive help if needed. Notice that the client continually mentioned, "I'm not crazy, I'm not nuts." It is a very common theme and concern of suicidal clients that their thoughts may be symptoms of psychosis or severe mental illness. Reassurance and acceptance of the person's experiences are important. Helping them feel that they are not crazy and that their thoughts and feelings are understandable also lessens the client's feelings of social isolation and emotional despair.

After this interview, the therapist wrote the following assessment note to summarize the prior interview.

The patient presented with feelings of depression, anger, and frustration. He stated, "I'm just tired of all this pain and depression." A direct assessment of suicidal thoughts and plans revealed he had recurrent thoughts of suicide by jumping from the local dam. On one occasion, while drinking, he went to the dam to jump. After looking at a picture of his children, he did not complete his plans. His commitment to his children's future seems to be a major motivating force for continued efforts to cope. Presently the patient denies any specific intent to kill himself or a specific plan, time, or place. He assessed his interests in living as 81% currently versus 50% at the point of his visit to the dam. He was offered the opportunity for inpatient care, which he declined. Following this direct discussion, his affect improved slightly and he became more engaged in the interview.

The patient needs reassurance that his thoughts are not "crazy." Therapy would be directed toward improving his day-to-day functioning and planning new work and recreational activities that come within his physical limitations. Suicide risk will be reassessed weekly. We will monitor for unanticipated losses or stresses in his life, alcohol consumption, feelings of isolation and hopelessness.

At this time, the patient does not wish hospitalization. The risk of suicide is considered moderate based on his demographic characteristics and current clinical features. It will be important to establish hope and specific plans to help him move ahead in his life in the areas of work and social functioning.

SUMMARY

This chapter has presented a decision making model to organize and guide the assessment of the potential risk of suicide for a client. Proceeding from the most general to the specific, the data-gathering stage begins with the determination of the person's demographic profile and its comparison with known high- and low-risk demographic groups. In the second phase, historical and current situations and psychological factors are assessed and evaluated as they relate to suicide risk. If there are moderate- to high-risk historical and clinical factors present, then the therapist is encouraged to directly assess potential suicide risk through an interview. The suggested interview directly inquires about whether the person has current thoughts of suicide and specific plans to do so at this time. The method, the availability of method, and specificity of the time and place for the suicidal act are determined through the clinical interview. In addition, the client's reasons for living and attitude toward receiving help are assessed.

At the end of this stage, a therapist may wish to obtain additional information about the client's risk through the use of standardized self-report measures. These measures are highly suggested if the client presents with ambiguous information and/or is in the mild- to moderate-risk categories based on the earlier information. If a client already provides clear indices that he or she is at high risk, such as the presence of depression accompanied by alcohol abuse, a specific suicidal plan, and the completion of final arrangements, then the administration of self-report measures is not needed. Instead, the therapist should move immediately toward steps to protect the person's life and to engage him or her in intensive treatment.

The next chapter summarizes the available self-report measures that may provide useful additional information to assess the level of suicide risk. These measures are helpful to quantify some of the relevant clinical dimensions, such as hopelessness and hostility, and to compare an individual's scores with normative groups. In clinical decision making, the more independent sources of information that converge and offer the same opinion, the more confident the therapist can be in the ultimate decision making. Therefore, if the information summarized in this chapter does not yield a clear and consistent profile of either no or high suicide risk, then the therapist is strongly encouraged to consider administering the instruments in the next chapter.

Chapter 5
Assessment by Self-Report

Following the initial assessment phase presented in Chapter 4, the mental health professional must determine whether the client presents low, moderate, or high risk for suicidal behavior. In cases where risk appears mild to moderate, or is unknown, the use of standardized assessment instruments facilitates a comprehensive evaluation of relevant clinical dimensions.

Self-report instruments are especially valuable in assessing a client's cognitive and affective states. Risk factors such as depression, hopelessness, and hostility are important in determining risk level. This chapter presents an introduction to some of the available instruments for relevant clinical dimensions in the assessment of suicide risk. The instruments were chosen primarily for their clinical utility, in that they provide clinically significant information, are psychometrically sound, and can be efficiently administered, scored, and interpreted.

It must be noted that self-report instruments should never be used as the sole criterion to determine risk level. The devices discussed below should be used in conjunction with converging information from interviews, direct observation, and collateral others. The therapist should strive to gather information from a variety of sources, using various methods.

The use of self-report inventories requires at least minimal reading skill of approximately sixth-grade level. If necessary, the instruments described below may be verbally administered to clients.

DEPRESSION

Depression is the clinical dimension most commonly associated with suicidal behavior. In fact, one study (Murphy, 1985) found 80% of completed suicides were committed by people who were depressed at the

time. Although many suicidal persons are not depressed, the significant portion of depressed individuals who are suicidal requires that the
therapist assess depression as part of a thorough evaluation.

Both severity and chronicity of depression should be considered when
evaluating suicide risk. Symptoms of depression include

1. depressed mood along with
2. poor appetite or overeating
3. insomnia or hypersomnia
4. low energy or fatigue
5. low self-esteem
6. poor concentration or difficult decision making
7. hopelessness
8. recurring thoughts of death and/or suicidal ideation (DSM-III-R, 1987)

Utilizing a self-report method, as described below, allows the therapist
to evaluate the client's private events (such as thoughts and feelings)
while assessing behavioral indices of depression as well. The measures
described below represent only some of the potentially useful self-
report instruments. These represent our preferences based on familiarity with them and do not imply that they are empirically superior to
other instruments not reviewed.

Beck Depression Inventory

The Beck Depression Inventory (BDI) was designed as a self-report
instrument to assess the presence and severity of depressive symptoms. The scale consists of 21 groups of items that correspond to the
cognitive, affective, motivational, and vegetative characteristics of
depression. Clients select one statement from a group of four statements that best describes their feelings for the preceding week, including the day they complete the inventory. For example, one group of
statements concerning the affective component of depression includes
the following items: "I do not feel sad; I feel sad; I am sad all the time
and I can't snap out of it; I am so sad or unhappy that I can't stand it."

Psychometric properties of the BDI have been extensively researched. The instrument has been demonstrated to have high internal
consistency, and test–retest reliability for various populations has been
very good. In addition, the instrument has been shown to correlate
highly with other measures of depression. Finally, the inventory's sensitivity to changes during treatment has been shown.

Each response is weighted on a scale from 0 to 3. Scores for each
item are summed, resulting in a total score. The possible scores range
from 0 to 63, with higher scores representing many depressive symp-

toms of greater severity. Extensive research has been conducted with several clinical and nonclinical populations, yielding normative data for a wide variety of populations. Levels of depression, based on obtained BDI scores, are presented below (Shaw, Vallis, & McCabe, 1985).

0–9   Normal nondepressed state
10–15   Mild depression
16–23   Moderate depression
24–63   Severe depression

Shaw et al. (1985) also suggest the following interpretations of post-treatment BDI scores:

0–9   Depression in remission
10–15   Partial remission
16–63   Presently symptomatic

The BDI is extremely useful in the clinical assessment of depressive symptoms when considering risk for suicide. The inventory is easy to administer and score. The extensive research literature indicating sound psychometric characteristics supports its use as a valid and reliable instrument. The inventory can be used throughout treatment as a dependent measure, as well as for continuous monitoring with clients who present mild or ambiguous risk.

The BDI is available from The Psychological Corporation, 555 Academic Court, San Antonio, Texas 78204.

HOPELESSNESS

As a result of the extensive research on depression and suicide by Beck, Kovacs, and Weissman (1979), hopelessness has been identified as one of the core characteristics of both pathologies. In fact, Beck et al. have found hopelessness to be a better correlate of suicidal ideation than depression. This finding resulted from investigating the hypothesis that the statistical association between suicidal intent and depression is an artifact that results from their common relationship to the variable of hopelessness.

Hopelessness Scale

Beck, Weissman, Lester, and Trexler (1974) designed the Hopelessness Scale to evaluate a person's negative expectancies. The scale consists of 21 items that are concerned with an individual's evaluation of the self and his or her future. Clients are asked to respond to true or false statements such as "There's no use in really trying to get something I want because I probably won't get it" and "I can look forward to more good times than bad times."

The Hopelessness Scale has demonstrated validity and reliability. Perhaps most importantly, Beck and colleagues have empirically demonstrated the predictive utility of the Hopelessness Scale for identifying persons who eventually commit suicide. Beck, Steer, Kovacs, and Garrison (1985) completed a prospective study in which they found a score of 9 or above predicted 91% of the eventual suicides in a hospitalized population (N = 165). In an additional study, Beck (1986, as cited in Beck, Brown, & Steer, 1989) found that a score of 9 or above successfully predicted 94% of suicidal persons from an outpatient population followed over a 6 year period.

Keyed responses are weighted 1 point, and points are summarized to yield a total score. The total score is then interpreted within suggested cutoff scores based on empirical investigation.

0–2 None or minimal hopelessness
3–5 Mild hopelessness
6–8 Moderate hopelessness
9+   Severe

The Hopelessness Scale is easy to administer and score. As a result, the instrument can be used clinically in the assessment of hopelessness as it relates to suicide risk. The scale may be used as part of initial assessment, as well as throughout treatment. It may also be useful as an outcome measure for the effectiveness of therapeutic intervention. Given the extensive amount of research indicating the significant relationship between hopelessness and suicidal ideation, the clinician should consider hopelessness as a clinical dimension critical in suicide risk evaluation.

The Hopelessness Scale may be obtained from Aaron T. Beck, MD, Center for Cognitive Therapy, 133 South 36th Street, Room 602, Philadelphia, PA 19104.

OTHER CLINICAL DIMENSIONS

Additional self-report instruments are useful in the assessment of relevant clinical dimensions when evaluating a suicide risk. Clinical risk indicators, as described in Chapter 4, are essential in a comprehensive evaluation. The following instruments allow the clinician to consider dimensions such as self-evaluation, hostility, and reasons for staying alive.

Suicide Probability Scale

Cull and Gill (1982) developed the Suicide Probability Scale (SPS) as a self-report measure to facilitate the prediction of suicidal behaviors. The scale is intended for use with adolescents (age 14 years and older) and adults. The instrument consists of 36 items rated on a 4-point Likert-type scale, requiring approximately a fourth-grade reading level. The client indicates the frequency with which she or he has experienced a specific emotion or behavior by selecting scale anchors ranging from "None or a little of the time" to "Most or all of the time."

Four empirically derived subscales representing current theories for predicting suicidal behaviors are contained within the scale. Items comprising Hopelessness subscale, for example, include "I feel so lonely I cannot stand it," and "I feel I can't be happy no matter where I am." The following scales are included:

Hopelessness (12 items)
Suicide ideation (8 items)
Negative self-evaluation (9 items)
Hostility (7 items).

Scoring the SPS is quick and easy as a result of the scale's format. Once the client has responded to all items, the therapist removes a top sheet, revealing the bottom page where response weights are indicated. Item responses are then summed, yielding a total score. In addition, subscale scores are computed by summing the response weights for keyed items.

Other characteristics of the instrument make it especially useful in clinical settings. The Rating Form includes space for the therapist to indicate the following information:

1. Demographic data. The client provides gender, age, and marital status, education, race, and occupation information. She or he also lists any major upsets or stresses that have occurred in the past 2 years.
2. Life events. The therapist is instructed to list recent psychosocial stressors, along with a severity rating of each stressor. In addition, the client's previous history of suicide attempts is recorded.
3. The therapist also records the presence of indicators for a major depressive episode, including dysphoric mood and other depressive symptoms.
4. Summary information. Once responses are scored, there is a small square on the front of the form in which to indicate (a) the total weighted score, (b) the T-score, (c) the probability score, and (d) the suicide risk rating.

The profile form is completed by the therapist once the client has responded to all items. The form includes space to record raw scores and total scores for each of the 4 subscales. There is a profile on which to record subscale scores and the total weighted score (i.e., the sum of all subscale scores). T-scores are indicated on the profile and facilitate interpretation of raw scores. The T-score and probability score for the total weighted score are derived from information listed in the corresponding manual's appendix. Thus, the SPS is particularly helpful in prompting the therapist to collect relevant information and to organize it in an efficient manner for clinical evaluation.

Ranges for interpreting probability scores are also included in the SPS manual. The following guidelines are suggested:

   0–24   Subclinical risk
   25–49   Mild risk
   50–74   Moderate risk
   75–100   Severe risk

The SPS is a clinically useful instrument in the assessment of suicide risk. The scale yields valuable information when responses to individual items are examined, as well as when subscale and total scale scores are used.

The SPS is available from Western Psychological Services, Publishers and Distributors, 12031 Wilshire Boulevard, Los Angeles, CA 90025.

Reasons for Living Inventory

The assessment of "reasons for living" allows the clinician to evaluate an aspect of suicidal ideation that is often overlooked. A client's cognitions related to reasons preventing suicidal behaviors provides the clinician with invaluable information not only in the assessment of suicide risk, but also in the formulation of effective intervention strategies.

The Reasons for Living (RFL) Inventory was designed from the perspective that individual belief systems may serve as mediators of suicidal behaviors (Linehan, Goodstein, Nielsen, & Chiles, 1983). The self-report measure includes items that assess a person's beliefs and expectancies related to reasons for not committing suicide. Clients are presented with 48 items and are asked to indicate how important each item is in the decision not to kill themselves. Item responses are scored on a range from 1 to 6, with 1 representing "Not at All Important," and 6 indicating "Extremely Important." Factor analyses have identified six distinct subscales:

Survival and Coping (24 items)
Responsibility to Family (7 items)
Child-Related Concerns (3 items)
Fear of Suicide (7 items)
Fear of Social Disapproval (3 items)
Moral Objections to Suicide (4 items)

Psychometric properties of the RFL continue to be investigated. The instrument has been found to discriminate between suicidal and non-suicidal individuals. The inventory has also been shown to have moderately high internal consistency.

Scoring the RFL yields a total score, based on a mean of the summary of all weighted responses. In addition, subscale scores for each of the six scales are computed by calculating the mean of weighted scores for keyed items.

At this time, Linehan (1985) has provided normative data for clinical and nonclinical populations. While cutoff scores for the scale or subscales are currently unavailable, Linehan (1985) has suggestions for interpreting client responses. Her findings have indicated that the absence of strong positive reasons to live are most indicative of suicidal behavior. A therapist may examine the client's positive reasons by looking at responses to items included in the survival and coping beliefs, responsibility to family, and child-related concerns scales.

As stressed by Linehan (1985), the RFL allows the clinician to focus assessment on adaptive aspects of suicide risk—reasons preventing individuals from self-destructive behavior. Although the psychometric properties of the instrument continue to be investigated, clients' responses to individual items provide valuable information. Consequently, the therapist gathers information that could be effectively used in formulating treatment plans.

The RFL Inventory is available from Marsha M. Linehan, PhD, Department of Psychology, NI-25, University of Washington, Seattle, WA 98195.

SUMMARY

Once an evaluation of a client's demographic and clinical profiles has been completed, the therapist may elect to use standardized self-report instruments to gather additional assessment information. Such data may be especially helpful when the therapist is uncertain about degree of risk, or when there is some indication of risk for suicidal behavior. Clinical dimensions, such as depression, hopelessness, and hostility, have been associated with suicide risk, and should be ad-

Table 5.1. Suggested Interpretation Scores for Determining Risk Level

	Risk Level			
Self-Report Instrument	None to Low	Mild	Moderate	High
Beck Depression Inventory	0–9	10–15	16–23	24–63
Hopelessness Scale	0–2	3–5	6–8	9+
Suicide Probability Scale	0–24	25–49	50–74	75–100

dressed as assessment continues. The Beck Depression Inventory, Hopelessness Scale, and Suicide Probability Scale offer a variety of empirically validated tools for the therapist. Table 5.1 summarizes the interpretation of these measures. The Reasons for Living Inventory provides a useful instrument for examining a person's reasons for not killing themselves, and as such, provides valuable information for risk evaluation and treatment planning.

As scores on the various instruments converge with information previously gathered, the therapist is able to assess risk level. Risk for suicidal behavior should be considered high when scores on the above instruments are consistently in the moderate to high range. Also, convergence of low scores on the instruments, when considered with regard to their assessment information, indicates minimal risk. Thus, the therapist's confidence in determining risk depends on the consistency of available information. When all self-report measures indicate a high level of distress, risk can be considered severe. However, the therapist must also be aware that if only one index of distress is high while others are low to moderate, the client may still present with considerable risk. Information from interviews and consultation with collateral others may be particularly critical in these cases. Finally, in cases where risk is unclear, therapists will do well to exercise caution. That is, assessment should be continued and responses should be based on the therapist's judgment of intent, means, availability, and lethality of suicidal expression (see Chapter 7). In cases where clients present clear risk for suicidal behavior, the therapist may elect to forego further assessment and proceed with interventions as described in Chapter 8.

Chapter 6
Child and Adolescent Suicide

Suicidal behavior among children and adolescents presents the mental health professional with a number of special concerns for both assessment and treatment. Several age-related needs and characteristics distinguish suicidal youths from adults. This chapter provides the clinician with information necessary to assess young individuals for suicide risk.

Parents, mental health professionals, and school personnel all have become increasingly aware of the risk and incidence of suicide among adolescents. In fact, suicide has been identified as the third leading cause of death among adolescents (following accidents and homicides) (Holinger & Offer, 1984). Each year in the United States, approximately 6,000 people under age 19 commit suicide (Greene & Keown, 1986). Suicide rates among youths ages 15 to 19 increased by an alarming 400% from 1950 to 1977 (Eisenberg, 1984).

In a recent epidemiological study, Holinger and Luke (1984) identified patterns of suicide among youths. Rates were found to be higher for males and whites than for females and nonwhites. Rates tend to increase from early adolescence and level off at the mid-20s.

While occurrences of adolescent suicide have been widely publicized, suicidal behaviors among children as young as 5 years also have been reported. The identification of self-inflicted death among children has been especially problematic. Self-inflicted death among children may not be accurately reported, due to a number of factors. These include social and religious stigma, family concerns and efforts to conceal causes of death, along with disagreement about the ability of young children to intentionally inflict self-harm (Pfeffer, 1986). National statistics indicate that 255 children ages 5 to 14, and 5,120 young adults ages 15 to 24 committed suicide in 1986 (National Center for Health Statistics, 1988).

Regardless of the exact prevalence of completed suicide among children and adolescents, therapists must be knowledgeable about the clinical assessment and treatment of suicide risk in youths. Efforts at prevention rely predominantly on an ever-increasing skill and knowledge in assessing high risk individuals. This chapter is intended to familiarize the mental health professional with current information regarding the evaluation of youths for suicide risk.

The authoritative text on the assessment and management of suicide among children has been written by Cynthia Pfeffer (1986). The book includes an extremely thorough review of the current assessment and treatment literature and offers detailed suggestions. Those readers who work with children and adolescents are encouraged to consult Dr. Pfeffer's definitive text for a comprehensive and detailed discussion of the issues most relevant to the management of suicidal children. Many of Dr. Pfeffer's helpful suggestions have been included in the following discussion.

DEVELOPMENTAL CONSIDERATIONS

Two age-related issues hold particular importance in the discussion of suicide risk among children and adolescents: the development of language and concepts of death. The assessment of suicide risk relies heavily on the child's ability to communicate thoughts and feelings about life and death. The therapist, therefore, must be familiar with age-appropriate language in order to ask questions the child is likely to understand and answer. Children between the ages of 3 and 6 think in very concrete terms and are just developing the ability to think back to past events, anticipate the future, and reflect on current events. Often, children may represent thoughts and feelings through symbolic play by making one object stand for something else.

The child's ability to communicate improves with the ability to consider other points of view, typically developing around age 7. Children begin to take many aspects of a situation into view, rather than focusing on one aspect only when drawing conclusions. Children do not develop an ability to think at higher levels of abstract reasoning until adolescence. At that time, they begin to consider many possibilities in situations and can engage in hypothetical reasoning, allowing them to go beyond what is seen in concrete terms to consider all possibilities that may exist in a situation. Adolescents do, however, continue to focus on what they believe will happen in a particular situation, often failing to recognize the concrete consequences of their actions. For example, Elkind (1967) described the "personal fable," referring to adolescents' beliefs that they are somehow special, and as a result are immune to harm. Often, teens who engage in dangerous and potentially self-destructive behavior believe they are protected from the naturally occurring consequences of such actions.

When asked specifically about death and related concepts, children express various beliefs at different age levels. Up until age 7, death is considered to be a temporary state. After about age 10, death is still considered temporary, and may be personified in various forms. Around age 13, children begin to express the understanding that death is final and irreversible (Koocher, 1974).

While many children typically express similar concepts of death at given ages, other factors influence the development of individual beliefs. They include levels of cognitive ability, emotional development, and personal experience with previous losses (Melear, 1973, as reported in Pfeffer, 1986). Suicidal children, however, often conceive death as temporary and as a pleasant condition that alleviates stressors (Pfeffer, 1986).

RISK FACTORS AND CLINICAL INDICATORS

Assessment of suicide risk requires knowledge of characteristics and behaviors associated with suicidal children and adolescents. Historical-situational factors and current psychological characteristics, and their relationship with suicide risk are described below. Table 6.1 summarizes the historical-situational factors while Table 6.2 lists the psychological characteristics to be considered in risk evaluation.

HISTORICAL-SITUATIONAL RISK FACTORS

Demographic factors, sometimes useful in assessing initial risk presentation among adult clients, have little value in the assessment of children and adolescents. The preferred course is to assess the interaction between environmental conditions and individual characteristics. Described below are the historical and situational factors that contribute to suicide risk in the young client.

Table 6.1. Historical-Situational Factors for Child-Adolescent Suicide Risk

	Low	Moderate	Severe
Medical history	Physically healthy	Minor health problems; adequate resources for care and emotional support	Chronic and debilitating illness; little to no emotional resources
Concepts of death	Age-appropriate and realistic	Temporary interest in death related topics; age-related fantasies and misconceptions	Chronic preoccupation with death and related issues; death romanticized and glorified
Specific skill deficits	No or minor impairment	Some impairment; no alternative skills	Severe impairment
Academic performance	Average to good	Some difficulties	Repeated failures
Peer relationships	Social with peers	Few available peers	No peer social network
Family system	Few to no stressors; adaptive parental coping	Few family stressors	Severely dysfunctional family system; severe discord; numerous stressors
Life stressors	None to some	Relatively infrequent	Unexpected, frequent, or chronic; major stresses such as death or divorce
Parental violence and sexual abuse	None	Disclosed incidents; treatment underway	No disclosure, no treatment; repeated occurrences
Parental psychopathology	Average affective state	Some parental distress; appropriate parental response	Parental psychosis; suicidality; chronic, chronic/severe depression
Family history of suicide	None	One or more distant relatives attempted or completed	Parental suicide behaviors
Dangerous behaviors	None	Infrequent and mild	High frequency risky behavior and harmful "accidents"
Previous suicide attempts	None	Infrequent, low lethality past attempt(s)	Recent and frequent attempts of potential lethality

Medical History

Though a common antecedent to suicide among adults, physical illness is not considered a primary factor in child and adolescent suicide. However, physical illness may decrease the individual's ability to effectively cope with other stressors.

Concepts of Death

Pfeffer (1981) reported that children's thoughts about death may be instrumental in their ability to deter suicidal actions. Young children often regard death as a temporary and reversible state that may be desirable as a means to terminate unendurable distress. Extreme stress may alter the thoughts of even those children who do understand the finality of death.

Preoccupation with death and related themes may be evidenced in statements, music, or jokes, and when chronic, should be considered serious. Finally, recent clinical observations suggest a relationship between involvement in satanic cults and self-destructive behaviors. Although very little empirical information is available, it appears that some adolescents may be involved in ritualistic behaviors that include self-mutilation and other self-destructive acts.

Specific Skill Deficits

If the child has inadequate coping mechanisms, or is in some way prevented from utilizing effective problem-solving skills (e.g., as a result of language difficulties), risk is increased.

Academic Performance

Repeated failures in the school environment may contribute to diminished feelings of self-esteem and escalate feelings of hopelessness. School may be considered (by parents as well as the youth) as a means of evaluating self-worth. Just as adults often define themselves in terms of specific roles (e.g., lawyer, mother), children may be perceived in relation to their success in the role they fulfill as a student.

Peer Relationships

Absence of a reliable social network of same-age peers, along with a lack of familial support may predispose the child to risk. Social and physiological developmental challenges of adolescence may prove overwhelming without a social network from which to obtain support.

Family System

Foremost among contributing environmental factors is the child's family system. Pfeffer (1981) has described several characteristics of families with psychiatrically hospitalized children that may be related to suicide risk. They include dysfunctional family organizations, severe marital discord, unusually enmeshed parent–child relationships, and rigidity. Children from severely dysfunctional families may be considered to be at increased risk for self-destructive behaviors. Families with ineffective communication and problem-solving skills are likely to model maladaptive responses to stress, such that the children adopt destructive coping mechanisms. A family system that ignores or aggravates a child's emotional distress increases the risk for maladaptive responding.

Life Stressors

Suicidal children have been found to experience a significantly higher number of life stresses during childhood than nonsuicidal children (Cohen-Sandler, Berman, & King, 1982). The stressors most commonly involved losses such as death and divorce. Other negative events, such as chronic illness or death of a family member, may increase risk when they occur unexpectedly, chronically, frequently, or within close temporal proximity.

Parental Violence and Sexual Abuse

Physical and sexual abuse are clearly associated with self-destructive behavior in children. Green (1978) found that such parental acts often were immediate antecedents to suicide attempts, threats, and behaviors among a sample of abused children.

Parental Psychopathology

Parents with severe emotional distress or histories of pathological behavior also have been associated with suicidal behavior among children. A history of suicidal behavior on the part of a parent or other family member predisposes a child to risk (Pfeffer, 1986). Children may learn that suicide is an acceptable way to deal with stress (Pfeffer, 1986).

One study (Tishler & McKenry, 1982) found that fathers of suicidal adolescents evidenced low self-esteem, depression, and alcoholism significantly more than fathers of adolescents who had not attempted suicide. In addition, mothers of attempters were more often alcoholic and had higher suicidal ideation scores than mothers of nonattempters.

Severe parental depression appears to predispose children to the development of affective disorders such as depression, along with separation anxiety disorders and attention deficit (Pfeffer, 1986). As a result, children of severely depressed parents may be considered at elevated risk for the development of disorders associated with suicidal behaviors.

Family History of Suicide

Suicidal behavior among parents has been found to correlate highly with risk for suicide among children and adolescents (Pfeffer, 1981). Parental modeling of suicidal behavior may result in children's learning maladaptive coping strategies in response to stress.

Dangerous Behaviors

Engaging in deliberately dangerous and risky behaviors, such as walking along the top edge of a highway overpass bridge, or speeding the wrong way down a one-way street, indicate risk for self-harm, as does a high frequency of accidents. Such behaviors may be considered an expression of intent to inflict harm on oneself.

Previous Suicide Attempts

People who have attempted suicide are at increased risk for eventual completed suicide. The frequency, lethality, intent, and recency of past attempts all indicate a level of current individual risk.

PSYCHOLOGICAL RISK FACTORS

Several characteristics comprising a child's current psychological state contribute to the overall level of suicide risk. Other clinical indications involve the client's behavioral repertoire.

Recent Losses/Separations

Loss may be experienced by both children and adolescents as a result of divorce, separation, death, or abandonment. Such loss often precipitates feelings of rejection, worthlessness, and loneliness. Losses experienced in early childhood are most often associated with completed suicides, while those experienced during adolescence are more often associated with suicide attempts.

Among adolescents, the termination of a significant relationship may precede suicidal acts. Such breakups may be very painful, and suicidal responses may be intended to end emotional pain or to attempt to influence the other's likelihood to return.

Table 6.2. Psychological Factors for Child-Adolescent Suicide Risk

	Low	Moderate	Severe
Recent losses/ separations	None	Few with adequate coping	Divorce; death; romantic break up
Depression	Average affect	Moderate	Severe; chronic
Hopelessness	Hope for future	Moderate	Severe; chronic
Psychosis	None		Present; hallucinations
Substance use	None	Infrequent use	Frequent, chronic use; loss of control
Suicidal plan	Undecided method; no available means; unclear lethality	Specific method; available means; moderate lethality	Method; time; place; high lethality
Final arrangements	None	Evident planning	Saying goodbye; giving belongings away

Depression

Depression is the psychological disorder most closely associated with suicidal behavior in both children and adults. Several studies (e.g., Carlson & Cantwell, 1982; Robins & Alessi, 1985; Shaffer, 1974) have found that among children and adolescents who engage in suicidal ideation and attempts, a high percentage experience severe depression.

Ryan et al. (1987) have described some differences between children and adolescents in their symptomatology associated with depression. Among clinically referred adolescents and children, adolescents were found to make suicidal attempts of greater lethality. However, there were no significant differences in rates of attempts, severity of ideation, or seriousness of intent. Notably, the state of being suicidal increased with increased duration of the depressive episode.

The severity and chronicity of depression appears to be a particularly significant risk indicator in the evaluation of suicide risk. Manifestations of depression vary among children and adolescents. Common symptoms of depression in childhood and adolescents are summarized in Table 6.3. Recognition of these symptoms is critical in the assessment of suicide risk. While not all depressed individuals are suicidal, the great majority of suicidal people experience depression. Hopelessness, a construct related to depression, is especially indicative of suicide risk and should be assessed accordingly.

Table 6.3. Symptoms Associated with Depression Among Children and Adolescents

	Children	Adolescents
Psychological Indicators		
Sleep disturbance	Difficult falling asleep or sleeping through the night; difficult or early awakening	Reversal of normal pattern—retiring early; rising early
Eating habits	Significant weight loss or weight gain	Loss of interest in food and eating
Motoric Changes		
Activity level	Marked increase or decrease in normal level of activity	Complacent
Social Interactions	Loss of interest in peers play	Withdrawn
Cognitive Changes		
Self-image and self-esteem		Feelings of worthlessness self-condemnation; impaired self-defense, pronounced self-deprecation

Caveat. Presence of any number of these symptoms does not necessarily represent depression; they may indicate a number of other child/adolescent problems. Presence of these symptoms must be considered within the context of collateral information.

Hopelessness

Feelings of hopelessness represent a very distinct and specific set of emotions and cognitions associated with suicidal behaviors. Feelings of despair, lack of control, and pessimism about the future are all indicative of the degree of hopelessness felt by individuals experiencing displeasure with their current lives.

In one study examining hopelessness and suicidal behavior (Asarnow, Carlson, & Guthrie, 1987), feelings of hopelessness were associated with increased suicidal behavior among children as young as 8 years. In addition, severity of depression was related to both hopelessness and suicidal behavior.

Thus, it is evident that a child or adolescent's view of the future and his or her role in it is a significant indicator of the degree of distress being experienced. As such, hopelessness is a critical dimension in the picture of suicide risk. The mental health professional must assess the client's expectations about the future to facilitate risk assessment.

Psychosis

As with adults, psychotic illness should be considered to heighten risk for suicidal behavior, particularly in the rare cases where command hallucinations are manifested.

Eating Disorders

Bulimia, considered by some to be behavior that is both destructive and impulsive, has been associated with heightened risk for suicide among adolescents with eating disorders (Chiles, 1986).

Substance Use

As with adults, alcohol and drug use may decrease inhibition and/or increase depressive affect. Chronic and excessive use of such substances substantially increases the risk for self-destructive behaviors. Substance use may reflect an individual's inability to use more adaptive methods to cope with stress.

Suicidal Plan

An individual's plan to commit suicide should be examined specifically in terms of means, availability, lethality, and intent. When these factors are present to some degree, risk should be considered moderate. In children and adolescents who disclose specific plans that include available and lethal means, risk should be considered severe.

Final Arrangements

At the extreme, youths who allude to not being present for future events, who say good-bye to friends with finality, and who give away favored or prized possessions should be considered at high risk. Such youths may appear unusually calm and contented, often as a result of having made a decision to act on the thoughts of ending their lives.

ASSESSMENT PROCEDURES

Beyond a thorough clinical evaluation of risk factors, the mental health professional should use various methods to complete a comprehensive assessment of suicide risk. These methods include paper-and-pencil self-report instruments, direct observation, and interview. The following section describes the use of these methods and provides a number of specific suggestions.

Self-Report Instruments

Self-report instruments may be especially valuable in the assessment of private events, such as thoughts and feelings about suicide and related issues. However, information gathered through self-report methods should never be the sole source for suicide risk assessment. Accuracy of self-report data may be influenced by intentional misrepresentation or perceived social desirability for responding in certain ways. In addition, young children may not possess adequate language and reading skills to ensure reliable responses. These shortcomings notwithstanding, a number of particularly relevant devices can be used to aid the professional in assembling a comprehensive evaluation.

The use of self-report questionnaires with children and adolescents to determine suicide risk is not as widespread as their use with adult clients. Indeed, the number of empirically supported devices for use with youthful clients is severely limited. There are, however, some instruments that professionals may find useful. As a prerequisite to using these instruments with any client, it is important to first determine the youth's ability to read and comprehend the instructions, items, and response choices. If necessary, the following instruments may be administered by reading items aloud to clients.

Children's Depression Inventory. Developed by Kovacs and Beck (1977), the Children's Depression Inventory (CDI) is one of the most widely used instruments for assessing the cognitive, affective, and behavioral signs of depression in children. The instrument was modeled after the Beck Depression Inventory, a self-report questionnaire that assesses depressive symptoms among adults.

The 27-item scale can be used with youths between 8 and 17 years. From a group of three statements, the client selects the one item that best describes him or herself for the preceding 2 weeks. For example, the following three items are grouped together: "I have trouble sleeping every night; I have trouble sleeping many nights; I sleep pretty well." Another symptom of depression is assessed via the following group of statements: "I am sad once in a while; I am sad many times; I am sad all the time." Based on the endorsed statement, a score of 0, 1, or 2 is assigned. Scores for each group of items are added together to obtain a total score. The total score represents the reported frequency and severity of symptoms as derived from the endorsed items. A higher score indicates endorsement of more severe and numerous depressive symptoms.

Extensive research on the psychometric properties of the CDI has contributed to the clinical utility of the instrument. The CDI has been demonstrated to distinguish between psychiatric and nonpsychiatric populations, and also correlates with measures such as hopelessness. The instrument has high internal consistency, and adequate test–retest reliability. Normative data are also available. The CDI continues to be empirically investigated, with additional focus on the stability of severity scores (Kazdin, 1988).

The CDI can be used as an initial measure to determine severity of depressive symptoms. In addition, it is a useful instrument for repeated measures throughout treatment, and as a posttreatment followup measure. The instrument may be obtained from Maria Kovacs, PhD, Professor of Psychiatry, Western Psychiatric Institute and Clinic, 3811 O'Hara Street, Pittsburgh, Pennsylvania 15261.

Hopelessness Scale for Children. The Hopelessness Scale for Children (HSC) was designed by Kazdin and colleagues (Kazdin, French, Unis, Esveldt-Dawson, & Sherick, 1983) to measure children's cognitions related to hopelessness. As with adults, assessing hopelessness is a critical component in the assessment of suicide risk. The degree of hopelessness may be a significant predictor of suicidal behavior for children. The HSC focuses primarily on the child's perceptions of the future, and thus provides information about the individual's expectations for his or her own life.

The HSC is a 17-item self-report inventory that can be used with children 7 years old and above. The instrument includes items to which the child responds either true or false, indicating whether or not the item describes how they feel. For example, the following items describe perceptions about their lives the child may or may not have experienced: "All I can see ahead of me are bad things, not good things," "Tomorrow seems unclear and confusing to me," and "I can imagine what my life will be like when I'm grown up." The instrument is scored by counting the number of scored responses that are in agreement with keyed items. Possible scores range from 0 to 17, and higher scores indicate greater degrees of hopelessness.

Extensive data regarding the psychometric properties of the HSC are not yet available. Scores on the HSC have been correlated with measures of depression, and have also been inversely correlated with self-esteem. The instrument has been shown to discriminate between suicidal and nonsuicidal children. The HSC may be used as one component of a diagnostic battery, and is appropriate for use throughout, as well as following, treatment.

The HSC can be obtained from Alan E. Kazdin, PhD, Department of Psychology, Yale University, P.O. Box 11A Yale Station, New Haven, Connecticut 06520-7447.

Suicidal Ideation Questionnaire. The Suicidal Ideation Questionnaire (SIQ) was developed by Reynolds (1987) specifically to assess adolescents' thoughts about suicide. As a result of extensive clinical contact with distressed adolescents, Reynolds noted that many adolescents engaged in suicidal cognitions, but did not present depressive symptoms. He then designed the SIQ to evaluate cognitions of death and suicide.

The 30-item SIQ is intended for adolescents in grades 10 through 12. The adolescent is asked to indicate the frequency with which specific thoughts occurred in the month prior to assessment. The instrument has been designed to include a variety of suicidal thoughts ranging in severity from mild to extreme. Sample cognitions in the SIQ included the following: "I thought about telling people I plan to kill myself," "I thought that my life was too rotten to continue," and "I thought about what to write in a suicide note." There are seven possible responses for each item, ranging from "I never had this thought" to "Almost every day." The scoring of the questionnaire is based on weights (from 0 to 6) assigned to each response category. The maximum score is 180, and higher scores indicate numerous suicidal thoughts occurring at high frequency. The total score may be compared with the criterion score (41 or above) suggested by Reynolds as a cutoff for clinical significance. Reynolds also urges mental health professionals to examine individual item responses for more specific information about patterns of suicidal ideation.

A shortened version of the SIQ, known as the SIQ-JR, to be used with adolescents in grades 7 through 9, has also been designed by Reynolds. The wording of the 15 items on the SIQ-JR is intended to be more appropriate for use with younger adolescents. For example: "I thought about when I would kill myself" and "I thought no one cared if I lived or died." As with the SIQ, the adolescent indicates the frequency with which each thought occurred in the preceding month. The scoring of the SIQ-JR is also based on a 0 to 6-point scale, with higher scores indicating greater frequency of numerous suicidal thoughts. The maximum score is 90, and the cutoff score for clinical significance is 31 or higher.

The SIQ and SIQ-JR have been standardized using relatively large samples. In addition, they have demonstrated high internal consistency and adequate test–retest reliability. In the absence of specific criteria for suicidal ideation, the content validity of the questionnaires has been demonstrated through relatively high item-total scale correlations. The SIQ and SIQ-JR have also been shown to correlate moderately with measures of depression, hopelessness, and anxiety, thus offering support for construct validity. Finally, normative data have been made available for both sex (male/female) and grade level (7 through 12).

Either the SIQ or the SIQ-JR may be used as screening devices for adolescent clients as part of a battery of general assessment. In addition, Reynolds recommends that the instruments may be used as screening devices on a large-scale basis, in that they are easily administered and scored. Toward that end, he recommends the use of the SIQ and SIQ-JR in junior high and high school settings. The SIQ is well-suited for use throughout treatment as a measure of treatment efficacy, as well as an outcome measure at time of termination or followup.

Both versions of the SIQ are commercially available from Psychological Assessment Resources, Inc., P.O. Box 998, Odessa, Florida 33556. In addition, William M. Reynolds, PhD, may be contacted at the Department of Educational Psychology, University of Wisconsin, 1025 West Johnson Street, Madison, Wisconsin 53706.

Collateral Report

Parents, siblings, peers, teachers, and others who have contact with the child may provide additional information for assessing risk. Individuals who have contact with the child in a variety of settings and roles should be interviewed to get a comprehensive picture about the child's characteristic behaviors in various situations. Responses to frustrations at school, peer relationships, and sibling interactions may be indicative of patterns related to suicidal thoughts and behaviors. Additionally, accounts of actual suicidal behaviors and verbalizations may be reported by others in the child's environment.

Significant others in the client's environment may provide information especially valuable in the formulation of functional analyses of suicidal threats and attempts. That is, individuals other than the client may be able to identify the variables contributing to specific incidents. Interviewing others helps to pinpoint the circumstances and conditions that led up to the suicidal behavior(s). The mental health professional can then begin to identify recurring or consistent patterns in the events leading up to a threat or attempt. Equally critical in such an analysis is an examination of the consequences that follow suicidal behavior(s). Those events also help the professional to determine the variables that serve to maintain suicidal behaviors.

For example, consider the following case: Every Saturday morning, 6-year-old Michael is expected to clean his room. Although he generally starts out by picking up his toys, within 10 minutes his mother hears him throwing his toys against the wall and screaming at them. At this time each Saturday, Michael's mother and father routinely argue about their financial situation while sitting downstairs paying their overdue bills. Upon hearing Michael's outburst, his mother runs upstairs to stop him. Michael usually throws himself on the bed, on the floor, and against the walls, while screaming, "I wish I could just kill myself. I'm going to do it, you know. And you'll be sorry." Michael's mother then pulls him onto her lap and spends the next half hour comforting him. Michael then leaves the room to play outside, because his mother has told him she'll finish cleaning his toys up. Michael's mother would rather send him outside to play than force him to clean his room, thinking that to do so would be too stressful given his upset condition. In the preceding few weeks, Michael's mother has reported that he tells her he wished he could die almost every day. According to his mother, Michael usually says that just before the family sits down for dinner each night. She usually responds by taking a few minutes to sit with him in his room and soothes him by rubbing his back, and telling him how hurt she'd be if something happened to him.

An analysis of Michael's threats indicates that these verbalizations typically occur when he's alone in his room, either on Saturday mornings or just before dinnertime. Also, during these times both of his parents are generally engaged in other matters, such as paying the bills and preparing dinner. Following Michael's threats, his mother leaves the task she's involved in to attend to Michael's needs. Thus, it appears that Michael's behaviors have become very functional for him, in that his mother typically responds by increasing her attention to his needs. Not only that, but Michael does not need to complete tasks like cleaning his room and is allowed to go outside to play with his friends instead. This example illustrates the possible progression of suicidal threats as a function of their effect on the significant others in the client's environment.

Consider the case in which 17-year-old Becky's boyfriend Carl had just left for college. Before leaving, Carl told Becky that he was planning to date other girls and that she should start dating others also. The first time Carl called her from campus, Becky was crying and told Carl, "I really don't think I can live without you. I haven't been able to stop thinking about you and wondering about the girls you're going to date. You're probably never going to come back to me." Carl attempted to comfort Becky, and promised to come home as soon as the first break was scheduled.

The next day in school, Becky told her best friend that she had been very upset about Carl, and that she had not been able to eat or sleep much since he had left for school. She also said that she'd been thinking about killing herself, since that was the only way she thought things would change for her. Becky's friend urged her to talk with her mother or the school counselor, but Becky refused. Her friend later went to Becky's mother to tell her she was worried about Becky, and about what she had said. Becky's mother immediately talked with Becky, who agreed to go to an appointment at the community mental health center. Based on clinical interview, the on-call worker recommended voluntary hospitalization in the adolescent unit of the local psychiatric hospital. Becky agreed and asked her mother to call Carl and tell him she had been hospitalized.

Upon hearing from Becky's mother, Carl left school and went home to see Becky. When he visited her, she seemed to be happy and not at all as down in the dumps as he had expected to find her. He spoke with Becky's therapist, who indicated that Becky was unlikely to harm herself, and that she would be going home within the next few days. Carl decided to stay until she was released and visited her each day, staying for all of the visiting hours. Upon her release, he agreed to spend the rest of the week at home, so he could make sure she was going to be all right. He also agreed that he would not date other girls.

After Carl returned to school, he and Becky talked on the phone each evening. Things appeared to be going well for Becky, and Carl had kept his promise not to date other girls. One night when Becky called Carl, his roommate told her that he had gone to dinner with one of the girls from one of his classes. When Carl called her back later that same night, Becky told him that she was thinking again about killing herself. Carl told her that he was not going to fall for her tricks a second time, and that he was sure she would be just fine. He told her that she should not call him again until she could stop talking about hurting herself. He tried explaining that he was very busy with his classes, and it was difficult for him to study when she kept bothering him. Becky hung up the phone even before Carl could say good-bye.

Two hours later, Becky's mother called Carl. She had taken Becky to the emergency room because Becky had cut her wrist with a kitchen knife. Her mother had found Becky sitting on the back porch of their home. Upon seeing the blood from Becky's arm, her mother rushed her to the emergency room. Becky asked that her mother call Carl right away and tell him that she needed him to come home.

The progression of Becky's suicidal threats to actual gestures provides an illustration for the clinical utility of complete functional analyses. Such analyses depend on gathering information from a variety of sources about the historical and situational antecedents prior to suicidal behaviors. Becky had experienced the loss of someone she cared about a great deal. Subsequent clinical interviews with Becky, Carl, and Becky's mother indicated that Becky's repertoire of coping skills was maladaptive, in that she had often used threats to coerce others. The importance of examining consequences of suicidal actions is also clearly shown when considering Becky's case. Her suicidal threats and gestures were clearly functional in getting Carl to come home to see her and to promise not to date others. On a subsequent occasion when threats were no longer functional, Becky attempted to get Carl to respond to her by elevating the degree of her actions, thus attempting a suicidal gesture. A complete assessment would reveal the patterns of Becky's behavior, along with the variables that shaped and maintained them. Such a comprehensive assessment is invaluable in risk evaluation and in subsequent treatment planning.

Direct Observation

Observation of unstructured play activities and interactions can provide additional valuable information in the assessment of suicidal thoughts and behaviors. Such observation may be especially useful with young children who have difficulty expressing emotions or cognitions. Patterns of self-destructive behaviors or repeated themes of death and dying that occur during play may be expressed through the use of puppets or dolls.

Pfeffer, based on observations of play patterns of suicidal and nonsuicidal children, has identified characteristics of play indicative of suicidal tendencies. According to Pfeffer (1986), the repetition of certain themes and the intensity of demonstrated affect distinguishes suicidal from nonsuicidal children. Suicidal children often show behaviors characteristic of children at a much younger developmental stage, expressed through repetitive actions of loss and separation. Suicidal children also engage in very reckless and dangerous types of play, often breaking, throwing, and destroying toys and play objects. In addition, suicidal children have been observed to act out very intensely sadistic and dangerous play sequences with "super-hero" (e.g., Batman) characters. Thus, the observation of play sequences can yield information about children to facilitate the suicide risk assessment.

The observation of social interactions with others may provide helpful information regarding social skills, affective state, and available support. The way in which the child interacts with the therapist allows for observations of the child's mood and characteristic behaviors. Extreme withdrawal, hostility, helplessness, and hopelessness may be observed and should be noted throughout the therapist's interaction with the child.

Finally, observations of the child when engaged in interactions with family members yields additional diagnostic information. Again, characteristic behaviors may be observed, and the therapist also has the opportunity to see parental and sibling responses to various child actions. Parents may demonstrate extreme disinterest, hostility, or an inability to attend to the child's emotional needs. Such observations yield invaluable information not only for diagnostic purposes, but also for the design of treatment plans.

The Clinical Interview

The interview is an essential part of diagnosing suicide risk. Often, therapists have difficulty completing such an interview with adult clients, and may find the process even more difficult with children. A number of issues and guidelines are discussed here to facilitate an efficient and thorough interview. Interested readers should also consult Pfeffer's (1986) book for discussion of the interview process.

The therapist should not avoid direct and frank discussion about suicide with a youthful client. It is necessary for determining the types of thoughts and feelings the child has concerning death in general, in addition to thoughts about his or her own life and death. However, care must be taken to use age-appropriate language with children. While using developmentally appropriate language, it is essential that the therapist ask the child directly about whether or not she or he has ever thought about hurting (or killing) him or herself. Children have the ability to respond to such questioning, often in a surprisingly open and direct manner. (Very young children may not be able to provide detailed information verbally; observations of play may be especially helpful in assessment, as discussed above.)

Following this questioning, the therapist should obtain a detailed account of the child's methods for completing self-destructive acts. As with adults, it is essential to determine the specificity of the child's plans, including information needed to determine intent and lethality. In addition, the therapist should assess the child's thoughts about what would happen as the result of completing a self-inflicted act; for example, what would happen to his or her family, his or her friends, and others. The therapist should also thoroughly explore the thoughts and feelings that preceded the suicidal thoughts and/or behaviors.

Any statement concerning death or intent to inflict self-harm should be considered seriously and thoroughly assessed. The frequency and depth of subsequent assessment should depend on the types of comments made by the youth.

Pfeffer and colleagues have developed a semistructured interview for the comprehensive assessment of suicide risk in children. The Child Suicide Potential Scales can be found in an appendix to Pfeffer's (1986) text and readers are urged to procure a copy of the interview format.

Several issues should be addressed by the therapist in the clinical interview. As with adults, the specific thoughts, feelings, and behaviors involved in the suicidal ideation or behaviors should be thoroughly delineated. The following transcript illustrates a sample clinical interview as conducted with a 7-year-old boy, and provides an example of the types of questions to ask when interviewing a young child.

Mark was brought to the community mental health center by his mother. She reported that Mark had been recently diagnosed as having a growth hormone deficiency, a condition that accounted for Mark's significantly small stature. In fact, his physician had informed Mark that he was a 7-year-old in a 4-year-old's body and his chances of achieving age-level height and weight without medical intervention were minimal. For the preceding three weeks, since the last meeting with his doctor, Mark had been engaging in anger outbursts at home during which he was telling his mother, "I wish I were dead."

Therapist: Mark, have you ever felt very, very sad?
Mark: Well, yeah, I feel pretty sad right now.
Therapist: Have you ever felt so sad that you thought you might hurt yourself?
Mark: What do you mean?
Therapist: Well, sometimes people feel really very sad and they think about doing things to hurt themselves. Have you ever thought about hurting yourself?
Mark: Yeah.
Therapist: When was the last time you thought about hurting yourself?
Mark: Last night.
Therapist: What were you doing when you thought about hurting yourself?
Mark: I was in my room.
Therapist: Where was your mother?
Mark: In the kitchen. It was after I finished my homework.
Therapist: How did you think of hurting yourself?
Mark: I wished I was dead.
Therapist: Did you think of killing yourself?
Mark: Yeah.
Therapist: Did you think about how you would kill yourself?
Mark: Yeah, I was going to get a knife from the kitchen drawer and cut my throat.
Therapist: Did you go to the kitchen to get the knife?
Mark: No.
Therapist: Did something stop you from doing that?
Mark: Yeah, my mom was in there and she won't let me get knives out of the drawer.
Therapist: Did you think of any other ways you might kill yourself?

Mark: Yeah, I thought about climbing in the tree just outside my house. It's real high and I thought I could just jump from the very top.

Therapist: Have you ever climbed to the top of that tree?

Mark: No, the lowest branch is way, way high above my head.

Therapist: Did you think of any other way you might hurt yourself?

Mark: Well, yeah, sometimes I go out to the road in front of my house and lay down in the street and wait for cars to come by.

Therapist: Have you ever done that before?

Mark: Yeah, I've done it lots of times. One time I even did it right when it was getting dark and people couldn't really see me.

Therapist: What happens when you lay down in the road?

Mark: My mom comes out and gets me.

Therapist: Have you ever done it when your mother wasn't home?

Mark: No.

Therapist: Mark, have you thought about what would happen if you died?

Mark: Yeah, I wouldn't have to worry about going to the hospital or about paying for the hospital bills.

Therapist: What do you think would happen to your mom?

Mark: I don't know.

Therapist: Do you think she'd miss you?

Mark: I don't know. Maybe.

Therapist: What do you think it's like when people die?

Mark: They go to heaven if they've been pretty good.

Therapist: What's it like in heaven?

Mark: I don't know.

Therapist: Do you think you'd be able to see your mom?

Mark: I don't know. [At this point, Mark began to cry.]

Therapist: Mark, you look like you're thinking about something that upset you. Tell me about what you were thinking just now.

Mark: My mom. I'd really miss my mom.

Therapist: I know your mom would miss you a whole lot.

Mark: I know.

Therapist: Mark, have you had any ideas about hurting yourself today?

Mark: No, I really haven't felt like that today.

Therapist: Tell me what you do feel like on the days you think about hurting yourself.

Mark: Well, I get mad at everyone and I just wish that they would leave me alone.

Therapist: It sounds like you're telling me that sometimes you get to the point where you just want to get away from everyone. Is that right?

Mark: Yeah, only people won't leave me alone and then I just get madder and madder.

Therapist: So you feel kind of frustrated when people bother you and you can't get them to leave you alone?

Mark: Yeah.

Therapist: When you feel frustrated, can you notice anything about the way your body feels?

Mark: What do you mean?

Therapist: Well, sometimes people can feel things change with their bodies when they're getting upset. When I get really angry, I notice that I

hold my fist real tight, like this. And then my whole arm starts to
shake. That's how I can tell that something's really bothering me. Can
you think of anything your body does when you start feeling really
frustrated?

Mark: Well, I sometimes start to breathe real heavy.

Therapist: That's good. That's just the kind of thing I mean when I talk
about the signals our bodies send us. When you start breathing heavier
than usual, you're beginning to feel very frustrated. Do you feel anything else different about your body when you get frustrated?

Mark: Yeah, my heart pounds so fast I think it's gonna jump right out.

Therapist: Okay, good. You start breathing heavier, and your heart feels
like it's pounding much faster. Those are both signs that give you a
message that you're feeling very frustrated. Let's talk about some things
you can do when you start feeling that way so that you don't get so
upset that you start thinking about hurting yourself. Okay?

Mark: Okay.

After all therapy sessions, accurate and comprehensive case notes
should be kept. Sessions that include an assessment of suicide risk should
be recorded with special attention given to details of the evaluation
that support the professional's determination of risk level. Specifically,
the professional must take care to note the assessment of the client's
present affective state, reported cognitions about suicide, and plans to
engage in self-destructive behaviors. The extent of the client's plans
should be described, with special attention to the means, availability,
and lethality. Finally, it is critical to note the safeguards that are present in the client's current living condition that allow him or her to remain in outpatient care. The professional must document the steps she
or he has taken to assure the client's safety. Documentation of the previous interview took the following form.

Case Note

Mark, a 7-year-old boy, was brought to the clinic today by his mother,
who reported Mark had been telling her that he "wished he were dead."
Mark has just been diagnosed as having a growth hormone deficiency,
which is responsible for his small stature. In addition, Mark's mother
reported that he has been engaging in several anger outbursts and appears to become easily frustrated with homework assignments and other
everyday household occurrences.

Throughout the interview, Mark presented himself as an extremely
quiet and polite young boy. He was quite willing to talk, and appeared
to answer all questions with sincere and well-formulated responses. Mark
admitted that he had been telling his mother that he wanted to die. Upon
further inquiry, Mark stated that he was very worried about his medical
condition and about the associated hospital expenses.

When asked about specific plans to hurt himself, Mark described three possibilities: (a) He would get a knife and cut his throat; (b) he would climb to a tall tree and jump; or (c) he would lie down in the middle of the street and wait for a car to run over him. Although he stated the first two were unlikely to occur, he did say that he had lain down in the road on previous occasions. His mother had come out of the house and retrieved him, and he reports never having done this when she was not at home.

When asked specifically about current thoughts or plans for harming himself, Mark did not report any. The feelings of frustration and anger that precipitate Mark's suicidal thoughts were discussed, and specific physiological antecedents (which included heavy breathing and increased heart rate) were identified to be used as cues for Mark. Strategies for decreasing Mark's arousal level were also introduced and included engaging in relaxation techniques. Finally, Mark agreed to inform his mother at any time he engaged in thoughts of self-harm.

The Children's Depression Inventory and the Hopelessness Scale for Children were administered. The score on the CDI was a 23, indicating a severe level of depressive symptoms. Mark's score on the HSC was a 7, representing a moderate degree of hopelessness about the future.

This therapist spoke with Mark's mother at the end of the session and advised her to remove all dangerous items from Mark's access. A review of such items indicated that his mother possessed a gun, from which she had removed all bullets and given them to a neighbor for safekeeping. In addition, a safe and inaccessible place for the storage of kitchen knives was identified (the locked cabinet over the sink). Mark's mother also agreed to increase her supervision of his activities at home, with special monitoring of his outside play. The importance of contacting the school about minimizing stressful events for Mark in the next few days was emphasized, and Mark's mother agreed to do so.

Before Mark left the session, he again agreed to tell his mother when he was feeling extremely upset and thinking about hurting himself. This therapist agreed that Mark's mother could then contact her at any time Mark thought or felt self-destructive. In addition, Mark and I shook hands to formalize the agreement, and then discussed the meaning of the agreement, and the importance of keeping promises that were sealed by handshakes. Mark's mother was given the local psychiatric hospital's crisis telephone number, along with his therapist's home phone number.

This therapist will phone Mark's mother this evening at 8 p.m. to be updated about the remainder of the days' events and to monitor any demonstrations of anger or frustration after school. In addition, I will contact the school this afternoon to arrange further assessment.

Tracey

The next interview was conducted with a 15-year-old girl who was referred for psychological evaluation following a second suicide attempt. Tracey's parents had recently divorced, and her 9-year-old sister had been placed in foster care due to her parents' inability to provide adequate care for her. Although Tracey was very close to her father,

her mother was granted custody of both Tracey and her 14-year-old brother.

Therapist: Tracey, the reason you're here today is because your mother and your caseworker are worried about you. They're concerned about your trying to hurt yourself.

Tracey: I don't have no mother.

Therapist: Tracey, your mom brought you here because she's been worried.

Tracey: I know. I know. My mother told me that's why I had to talk to you. So just go ahead. You talk.

Therapist: Well, I'd like to talk about what happened. Tell me about what you did to hurt yourself.

Tracey: I drank some Drāno.

Therapist: What happened right before you drank the Drāno?

Tracey: I had a fight with my brother. He came in my room and wanted to take my stereo.

Therapist: What happened after that?

Tracey: We started punching each other.

Therapist: Where was your mom?

Tracey: She wasn't home.

Therapist: Do you remember what time it was?

Tracey: About 12:15.

Therapist: During the day?

Tracey: No, at night.

Therapist: What happened after you started punching each other?

Tracey: I ran back to my room and Larry kept telling me he wished I was dead. So then I locked myself in the bathroom and decided that I'd give him his wish.

Therapist: Then what did you do?

Tracey: I looked under the sink and found the Drāno. I took a couple aspirin and then drank the Drāno.

Therapist: Do you know where Larry was?

Tracey: No, but it got real quiet in the house and I think he left.

Therapist: Then what did you do?

Tracey: I went outside and walked down to the edge of the apartment complex, down the hill by the woods.

Therapist: Could anyone see you?

Tracey: No, that's why I went down there. I just wanted everyone to leave me alone.

Therapist: Did you think anyone would find you there?

Tracey: No, I still don't know how my neighbor knew I was there. She was the one who called the ambulance. I don't even remember going to the hospital. The next thing I knew, I was there getting my stomach pumped.

Therapist: Tracey, can you tell me the reason you tried to kill yourself?

Tracey: I'm just so tired of fighting with Larry. He always makes me feel like I'm ugly and that I don't have any friends. He's always picking on me and telling me how much he hates me. Whenever I have my friends around, he really embarrasses me.

Therapist: Why did you feel that hurting yourself could change that?

Tracey: I thought my mom would listen to me. My sister got moved to a foster home and I just want her to come home. She's my best friend.

Therapist: Did you think that your sister might be able to come home if something happened to you?

Tracey: Well, no, but I thought my mom would listen to me if I did something.

Therapist: What would you want to tell your mom?

Tracey: That she and my dad should work at getting Julie home so everything could be the way it was before my dad left.

Therapist: Do you think that maybe your mom will talk to you about how you feel?

Tracey: She will now.

Therapist: What do you mean?

Tracey: Now she has lots of time to talk to me. She asks me how I feel all the time now.

Therapist: Do you think that's different than before?

Tracey: Yeah.

Therapist: How do you think it's different?

Tracey: Well, ever since I drank that Drāno, she's real interested in how I feel and what I'm doing.

Therapist: How has that changed?

Tracey: She never used to ask me about anything.

Therapist: Tracey, when was the last time you thought about killing yourself?

Tracey: The night I drank the Drāno.

Therapist: Have you had any thoughts about killing yourself since then?

Tracey: No, I really haven't had much of a chance to.

Therapist: What do you mean?

Tracey: I'm never really alone at home anymore since then.

Therapist: Have you had any thoughts about hurting yourself today?

Tracey: NO! I just told you I haven't wanted to do that for a long time.

Therapist: It sounds like you're upset that I asked you about whether or not you're thinking about hurting yourself.

Tracey: No, it's just that I really am tired of having everyone keep bugging me about it. I really only did that so my mom would just change things around.

Therapist: Tracey, what kinds of things are different now that would keep you from hurting yourself?

Tracey: Well, like I told you, my mom's been pretty good about staying home and talking to me.

Therapist: That's good. What other kinds of things are there now that keep you from hurting yourself?

Tracey: I have a lot more friends now. Some of the people who live next door have really been nice ever since they found out what I tried to do.

Therapist: So now you feel like you have someone to talk to when you're feeling really angry or upset, or just down in the dumps.

Tracey: Yeah, I've been going over there to my neighbors a lot.

Therapist: Have you thought about any other things that would keep you from killing yourself?

Tracey: Well, if I killed myself then my sister Julie wouldn't have anybody left.

Therapist: How do you think Julie would feel if you killed yourself?

Tracey: I think she'd be really sad. I was always the one to take care of her at home. And when she came home, she'd probably have a real hard time. Larry's pretty mean to her, too.

Therapist: So it sounds like you have more people to talk to when you're feeling bad, and that you've really thought about what it would mean for Julie if you killed yourself. Tracey, I'd like to ask you to do something when you're feeling bad and thinking about hurting or killing yourself, okay?

Tracey: Depends on what you're going to say.

Therapist: What I'd like to ask is when you're thinking about hurting or killing yourself that you take a minute before you do anything and think about some things. I'd like you to think about Julie and about your mom. And the other thing I'd like you to do is to tell someone before you do anything. Do you think you'd be able to do those things?

Tracey: Yeah, I think I'll be able to. That's kinda like what I've already been doing when I go talk to my neighbor.

Therapist: That's really good, Tracey. And if you ever have anything you feel like you can't talk with your mom or your neighbor about, then you can always call me or have your mom call, okay?

Tracey: Yeah, I guess so.

Therapist: Good. Tracey, I'd like to call your mom in now and tell her what we agreed on. Is that all right with you?

Tracey: Yeah.

Again, it is critical that the mental health professional provide an accurate and comprehensive description of the clinical interview. The interview with Tracey was summarized as follows.

Case Note

Tracey, a 15-year-old female, was brought in by her mother for evaluation (as recommended by Jane Butz, Department of Human Services caseworker). Tracey attempted suicide last Thursday (7/27/89) by ingesting several aspirin and Drāno. She required treatment in the emergency room, including having her stomach pumped. Currently, both Tracey's mother and caseworker fear that she is at risk for future suicidal behaviors.

Tracey described her suicide attempt as follows: She and her brother were involved in an argument late Thursday night. Their mother was not at home, and the verbal argument escalated into a physical fight. Following the fight, her brother told her repeatedly that he wished she were dead. She then went into the bathroom, ingested a handful of aspirin, and drank some Drāno. Tracey then left the house and walked to the outside of the complex where her family's apartment is located. She lay down on the grass in what she described as a secluded and wooded area. One of her neighbors found her there and called an ambulance. She was taken to General Hospital, where her stomach was pumped and she was sent home.

At times throughout the interview, Tracey seemed hostile and negative toward her mother. She also reported a severely strained relationship between her brother Larry and the other family members. Tracey was coherent, oriented, and did not report any delusional thoughts or hallucinations. She appeared rather tense, in that she constantly bit her fingernails and shook her leg while sitting in the chair. At the start of the interview, Tracey said, "I don't have no mother." Later in the session, she reported her mother as having changed the amount of time they spend together talking and at home.

When asked about reasons not to kill herself, she emphasized her sister's reliance on her. She also stressed that she felt she had people available in her community for social support.

The following instruments were administered: Beck Depression Inventory, Hopelessness Scale for Adults, and the Reasons For Living Inventory. Tracey's scores on these instruments were 27, 5, and 3.5, respectively. Her score on the BDI indicates a severely depressed individual. However, her scores on the HSA indicates that Tracey does not consider her present situation as hopeless. Although she reports an intensely depressed affect, Tracey perceives promise for her future, and expresses a desire to experience good things in life. Her score on the RFL places her in a category of individuals who may be at mild to moderate risk for suicidal behavior. However, a high score (5.25) on the Moral Objections Subscale represents Tracey's expressed belief that suicide is not morally appropriate, and corroborates her denial of present plans to inflict self-harm.

Tracey's mother reported a history of noncompliance and severe hostility both at home and at school. Her mother also reported a pattern of temper outbursts that immediately follow any parental requests and/or commands. Her teachers have reported numerous physical confrontations Tracey has directed toward her classmates.

Tracey agreed that she would talk with her neighbor or her mother at times she was thinking about hurting herself. She also agreed to contact me if there were things she could not discuss with others. At the end of the session, Tracey explained our agreement to her mother. I also spoke with Tracey's mother about removing hazardous items from the home, increasing her supervision of both Tracey and Larry, and procuring treatment services for the family. I gave them the names and phone numbers of two therapists in their community (Joe Cujo and MaryAnn Garcia). Tracey's mother agreed to call one of them and arrange an appointment, and to call me back to inform me of when she would begin services. I gave Tracey's mother the number of the psychiatric hospital in their community (Chestnut Hills) and my after-hours number.

Tracey's history of impulsive and aggressive behavior (directed both at others and herself) places her at moderate risk for future suicidal behavior. It is not clear whether her present environment can provide adequate support to prevent future incidents of suicidal behavior. At the present time, she reports having people available for support if necessary, and also identifies her sister as an important reason not to kill herself.

SUMMARY

The previous discussion emphasizes the need for comprehensive and detailed assessment procedures. A professional and ethical assessment is the result of using a variety of methods (self-report, interview, and direct observation), along with as many sources for information as possible. Above all, it is essential that all indications of self-destructive behavior be directly and repeatedly assessed. Once suicide risk has been determined, the therapist must respond accordingly. Guidelines for managing varying levels of suicide risk among children and adolescents are provided in Chapter 10.

Chapter 7
Overall Determination of Suicide Risk

In working with a potentially suicidal client, gathering the necessary demographic, clinical and psychometric data are the first steps toward assessing an individual's suicide risk. As defined in the case laws, a mental health professional is responsible for having properly assessed the risk that a client potentially presents to him or herself and then to take appropriate action to protect the person from harm. The degree of dangerousness that a person presents can be conceptualized on a continuum from 0 (no danger of self harm) to 100 (certainty of self harm). While dangerousness can be viewed on a continuum, it is often divided into levels for ease in communication and conceptualization. Similar to the work of Cull and Gill (1982) on the Suicide Probability Scale, suicide risk is divided into four categories: low risk, mild risk, moderate risk, and high risk. The use of these four categories leads to different suggested actions for the mental health professional.

Step 5 of Figure 5.1 is the decision point at which the therapist combines the demographic information, clinical factors, direct interview data, and self-report measures to consider a client in one of the four risk categories. Unfortunately, there is no prediction equation that allows a therapist to empirically combine the information from the various sources to make this judgment. One reason for this is the fact that stable risk factors interact with unpredictable events, such as job layoffs, car accidents, and social rejection. The self-report measures do offer empirical cutoff scores for different categories of risk, but these are only offered as guidelines and must be considered in combination with other sources of data. Information from the direct interview, along with clinical indicators such as prior suicide attempts or recent feelings of hopelessness, must be incorporated into an evaluation of risk. Overall, the prediction of risk and dangerousness is a very difficult enterprise.

PREDICTION OF
DANGEROUSNESS

Mental health professionals are often asked to predict the dangerousness of an individual toward him or herself or others. These questions can emerge as part of a civil commitment assessment procedure, presentencing evaluation of a convicted felon, or in capital punishment cases. A judge or jury may be required to consider evidence of future dangerousness in deciding whether to impose the death penalty. In the Supreme Court case *Barefoot v. Estill* (1983), the American Psychiatric Association wrote a brief to the Supreme Court acknowledging the great difficulty in the accurate prediction of future dangerous behavior.

While most of the research on the prediction of dangerousness is focused on the danger of a person toward others, the ability of mental health professionals to predict dangerousness of a person to him or herself is also poor. There are several factors that make the accurate prediction of suicide risk difficult.

The major problem of accurate prediction is the base rate problem. The relatively low rate of suicide, even among special populations, makes any accurate prediction difficult because suicide is a relatively rare event and the prediction factors are not highly precise. Even in the high-risk group, such as people who have already attempted suicide, the future risk of death by suicide in the next year is 1 in 100 people. However, to accurately predict which 1 individual out of 100 people who has attempted suicide will die within 1 year is extremely difficult. As illustrated by Hawton (1987), if we wish to identify the 1% of people who will kill themselves within the next year from among 1,000 suicide attempters, we are attempting to identify 10 deaths among the 1,000 people. If the predictive tools are 80% accurate, an optimistic figure, then we would be able to correctly identify 8 of the 10 suicides. Unfortunately, in addition to these 8 correct predictions, an additional 192 individuals would probably be identified incorrectly as possible suicides since we have a 20% inaccuracy rate even in our relatively accurate system. Therefore, we would identify 200 people, of whom only 8 eventually will commit suicide. If intervention and prevention were done for all 200 then the 8 lives may be saved but the expenditure of resources would be high. In turn, two of the eventual suicides would have been missed.

The problems of predicting any event when there is a low base rate are not unique to suicide. With any relatively low rate behavior, it is extremely difficult to predict accurately on an individual basis. The predictions are more accurate on a group or collective basis. Unfortunately, this does not help the therapist with an individual client.

A second problem of assessment is the difficulty in applying general factors to individuals. The prior chapters have identified demographic, clinical, and self-report indices of risk. They have been validated by comparing groups of individuals who have displayed suicidal behaviors with groups who have not. What is being offered are general trends and risk factors. The sex, age, and race of an individual, while useful at a group level, is nothing that can be treated or prevented to lower the demographic risk factor. A therapist cannot make an elderly, white, single man at lower risk on these factors with any known intervention. Membership in that group should alert the therapist to potential risk because it is higher for that group but it is not a unique predictor of that individual's future behavior. In fact, the vast majority of that group does not commit suicide.

The time frame for prediction is also a problem. Most therapists are primarily concerned about short-term or imminent risk of harm. The ethical guidelines offered by the American Psychiatric Association and the American Association for Clinical Social Workers permit the violation of confidentiality if danger is imminent. The ability to predict foreseeable actions is even harder than predicting long-term actions.

Long-term risk factors, such as psychiatric conditions of schizophrenia, alcoholism, or depression, raise the lifetime risk of suicide. However, some of these risk factors may change over time through intervention and prevention. A chronic alcoholic may become abstinent and remain abstinent from alcohol through a successful treatment program. This may lower the person's risk of suicide from the 15% lifetime risk mentioned in Table 3.2. Other risk factors such as physical illnesses may improve over time, or conversely, the illness may progress and the person may deteriorate further. Thus, the type of physical disorder present at the time of prediction may change and, therefore, change its effect on future suicide risk.

One of the most ambitious studies of the prediction of suicide was conducted by Pokorny (1983). He studied 4,800 patients who were admitted to the inpatient psychiatric service of a Veterans Administration Hospital who were followed for a period of 4 to 6 years to determine subsequent suicide or apparent suicide behaviors. Sixty-seven of the 4,800 veterans committed suicide during a mean period of 5 years, a rate of 279 per 100,000 per year, 12 times the rate for male nonhospitalized veterans, and approximately 23 times the general population rate. In addition, 179 suicide attempts occurred within this group during the 5-year followup period.

Despite sophisticated discriminant analyses using a variety of historical, clinical, and self-report measures, only one half of the actual suicides could be identified accurately while misidentifying 1,206 false positives. Of the total group identified as those who would commit suicide, only 2.8% were identified correctly. Thus, 97 of 100 persons predicted to be suicidal were incorrectly identified. The most accurate prediction of this low base rate behavior was to predict that no one would commit suicide. This would lead to a 98.6% accuracy rate, but would fail to identify any of the 63 individuals who died within the next 5 years.

More recently, Motto (1988) examined demographic, environmental, and psychological variables to determine which were predictors of suicide within a time frame of 60 days. From a sample of 3,000 hospitalized patients ages 9 to 68 who were severely depressed or in a suicidal state, 38 committed suicide within 60 days of the assessment (1.2%). From 186 variables assessed, the following nine were identified as predictors of short-term risk among this already high risk group of hospitalized patients:

1. Prior psychiatric hospitalization
2. Contemplation of suicide by hanging or jumping
3. Severe, moderate, or questionable suicidal impulses
4. Divorced marital status
5. Threat of financial loss
6. Sense of being a burden to others
7. The interviewer having a mixed or negative reaction to the patient
8. Severe crying or inability to cry
9. Severe or moderate ideas of persecution or ideas of reference

The presence of any of the first four factors increased the risk of suicide three times within the next 60 days while the remaining factors increased the risk at least twofold. Motto reported that when four or more factors were present, 71% of the suicides were correctly identified while correctly excluding 81% of the nonsuicides. While this research is tentative and needs to be replicated with a new sample, the potential of developing a suicide checklist to use with a high-risk subgroup of already hospitalized patients is an exciting development. However, most potentially suicidal patients are not already severely depressed and hospitalized. Therefore, the prediction of their future risk may require additional measures and procedures.

Overall, this ambitious study illustrates the great difficulty in identifying specific individuals even when they are already members of high

Table 7.1. Dimensions of Suicidal Dangerousness

---

1. Imminence of behavior
   (immediately to never)
2. Target of danger
   (self, specific others, nonspecific-global)
3. Clarity of danger
   (time, place, method, opportunity)
4. Intent of behavior
   (death to communication of needs without wish to die)
5. Lethality of behavior
   (lethal to nonlethal)
6. Probability of behavior occurring
   (very high to none)

---

risk groups and for whom a variety of clinical and self-report data is available. This should keep mental health professionals humble about the state of our science in predicting such low-rate behaviors. However, this study cannot be used to justify ignoring risk factors when they are present and cannot be used to justify not taking appropriate action when risk is apparent.

DIMENSIONS OF DANGEROUSNESS

Dangerousness is a construct that can be conceptualized along six dimensions. Table 7.1 summarizes these dimensions.

Imminence of Behavior

The imminence or immediacy of the risk is probably the most important dimension to be considered first. If the risk is imminent, then actions must be taken immediately to lessen the risk and to protect the person from self-harm. If, however, the imminence is in the distant future, regardless of how clear or lethal it is—for example, death by gunshot wound on anniversary of the widowed man's wife's death 10 months in the future—then the therapist has time and options to pursue. The therapist may not be forced to take a drastic action such as involuntary hospitalization to help preserve the person's life at that time. Other options can be considered since the risk is not immediate.

Target of Danger

The target of danger is the intended victim or victims. Often suicidal ideation occurs in a context in which there are angry and hostile feelings toward others. Suicidal thoughts may be accompanied by homicidal thoughts to specific others or to people in general. Many mass murderers have ended their homicidal sprees with suicidal acts. In domestic disputes there are often tragic murder-suicide scenarios. The target of danger should be considered. If there is potential danger to others, then the Tarasoff guidelines, which require a duty to protect the potential victims in addition to the client, may apply.

Clarity of Danger

The more precise and specific a client is about what he or she intends to do, when he or she plans to do it, and where this will occur, the greater the dangerousness. In addition to the method, time, and place, the opportunity for the client to act on these plans should be assessed. For example, if the client plans on committing suicide by an overdose and has already begun to accumulate potentially lethal medications, then the clarity of danger is higher than if the client has taken no steps toward acquiring the means to overdose. The more specific and clear the person is about the intended actions, the higher the dangerousness.

Intent of Behavior

Most people who commit suicidal acts do not die and, retrospectively, are viewed as not intending to die. Beck, Schuyler, and Herman (1974), developed a suicidal intent scale. This 20-item scale assesses the person's wish to die prior to a suicidal act. Beck et al. reported that the correlation between suicidal intent and the actual medical danger in their series of attempters was low. Similarly, Fox and Weissman (1975) reported that the degree of suicidal intent was generally lower among self-poisoners than those who deliberately injured themselves by other means. However, the medical risk from the overdoses was higher than the lethality of the self-injury. Overall, the person's intention or motivation to die is a separate dimension from the actual means that is selected for the suicidal act. A contemplated or attempted suicidal act cannot be dismissed merely because it was nonlethal. The intent of the person must be assessed.

Lethality of Behavior

Actual lethality or probability of death from the act should be assessed as a separate dimension. Smith, Conroy, and Eller (1984) developed a 10-point Likert scale to assess the lethality of a suicidal behavior. The scale ranges from 0.0 (death is very highly improbable) to 10.0

(death is almost a certainty, regardless of the circumstances or interventions by an outside agent). Most of the people at this level die quickly after this attempt. Seven intermediate points on this Likert scale are offered. For example, a score of 2.0 suggests that "death is improbable as an outcome of the act. If it occurs, it is probably due to unforeseen secondary affects. Frequently the act is done in a public setting or is reported by the person or by others. While medical aid may be warranted it is not required for survival. They may receive medical attention but it is not necessary." A score of 8.0 suggests that "death would ordinarily be considered the outcome to the suicidal act unless saved by another agent in a calculated risk. One or both of the following are true: 1) makes no direct communication, 2) takes action in private (major, quick blood loss, lethal overdose, and no communication)." The higher the lethality of the anticipated behavior, the more serious the risk. Appendix A contains the lethal dosages of the common prescription medications. This information can be helpful in assessing the potential lethality of an overdose attempt.

The Probability of Suicide Occurring

Overall, the therapist weighs the above five dimensions and arrives at a judgment as to the probability of a person acting in a dangerous way. While the empirical literature demonstrates the great difficulty in accurately predicting an individual's future behavior, a therapist still must exercise reasonable judgment and provide a clinical estimate as to the probability of the dangerousness occurring. Case laws do not require the clinician to be correct, as in *Johnson v. the United States* (1981) or *Paradies v. Benedictine Hospital* (1980), but do require the clinician to have shown reasonable judgment in arriving at the decision.

A model for the prediction of dangerousness to both self and others has been developed by Hall (1987). This model is based on the following assumptions: (a) Violence is the interaction of the person, the context or setting, and the potential victim, and not just a characteristic of the person alone; and (b) specific behaviors such as danger to others or suicidal acts are the interaction of the person with the environment in a specific time, place, and setting. Hall offers an eight-step series of issues that must be addressed before offering a prediction of dangerousness. Table 7.2 summarizes these.

First, the appropriateness of the referral is considered. Is the referral question appropriate for this therapist to address? If the question is about one's own client, it is clearly appropriate. However, if it is a question, for example, from someone in an audience at a lecture about another professional's patient, then the referral question may be inap-

Table 7.2. Hall's Violence Prediction Process Issues

1. Appropriateness of the referral
2. Adequacy of the data information base about the client
3. Bias or distortion of the client
4. History of prior violence by the client
5. Presence of triggering stimuli
6. Presence of an opportunity for violence
7. Presence of inhibitory factors
8. Prediction time-limited to the specific person and environmental factors (triggering opportunity v. inhibitory factors)

Source. Violence prediction by H. V. Hall, 1987. Springfield, IL: Charles C Thomas. Copyright 1987 by Charles C Thomas.

propriate and not answered. Second, the establishment of an adequate data base of both demographic and clinical indicators about the client is needed. Third, the biases and/or distortion of the client should be considered. A tendency to be deceptive or to malinger should be carefully evaluated (see Rogers [1988] for detailed discussion of malingering). Fourth, a historical analysis of the baseline for the individual's prior violence should be examined. Generally, the best predictor of future behavior is previous behavior. In the assessment of suicide risk, the best predictor of a future attempt may be the presence of a prior attempt. Gathering this information is critical. The fifth step involves identifying the antecedent or triggering stimuli that may incite the violent act. There are immediate stimuli of high intensity such as intoxication or a marital fight that may trigger a violent act. Knowledge about triggering events before a prior attempt would help assess whether these antecedents exist in the present situation.

The sixth step assesses the specific environmental factors that create the opportunity for the dangerousness to occur. Often opportunity variables are all or none. For example, a suicidal person will use a gun if available, but would not consider attempting suicide by using a knife if a gun were not present. The seventh step is the assessment of factors that may inhibit the acting out of the violence. These "buffer" factors, such as presence of a social support system or reasons for hopefulness, must be assessed.

The final step of this prediction process is the offering of a cautious, time-limited prediction. The prediction is time limited, because the person is assessed in the context of particular environment on a particular set of stressors when a specific opportunity and inhibiting factors apply. For example, a therapist may make the following prediction statement about his client [appropriate referral]. "The clinical interview combined with the Beck Depression Inventory and Suicidal Probability

Scale are all indicating moderate risk at this time [adequate database]. He has no prior suicidal attempts [history of violence]. The client is candid and not deceptive in his responses to standardized measures [distortion factor]. He is still optimistic that he may regain custody of his children [buffer factor], and a preferred means of death by a gunshot is not available since he gave his firearms to his brother-in-law [opportunity factor]. Furthermore, the client contracted that he would not do anything to harm himself before the next therapy session [inhibitory factor]. Overall, at this time he is not considered an imminent risk to harm himself but this must be reevaluated [time-limited prediction]." This example contains information about each of the elements suggested by Hall to make the replicable prediction of future dangerousness.

RESPONSES TO DANGEROUSNESS

If moderate to high risk of suicide exists, based on a combination of demographics, the clinical interview, and self-report measures, then the mental health professional should move immediately to determine the imminence of the risk. If the client presents with a high risk of suicide in the near future, then additional treatment is needed.

As summarized in step 6 of Figure 4.1, in the presence of imminent danger the therapist's first option is to consider whether intensified outpatient treatment is appropriate for the protection of the individual. If the probability of the suicidal behavior occurring is judged as low enough to warrant continued outpatient treatment, then treatment could continue on an intensified basis. Chapter 8 includes discussion on crisis management and therapy issues for maintaining suicidal patients on an outpatient basis. If, for a variety of reasons, outpatient treatment is not appropriate, then hospitalization is warranted. Before proceeding with either of these treatment decisions, the mental health professional should carefully review his or her own thoroughness, potential biases for or against forms of treatment, the needs of the particular patient, and the adequacy of the data base from which a decision is being made.

Whenever a client is at moderate to high risk for a suicidal act, it is strongly suggested that the therapist discuss the treatment decisions with an experienced colleague and document this discussion. This reflects sensitivity to the complexity of these decisions and an awareness of the value of additional input. While failure to obtain a consultation is not negligent, the use of a consultation shows further sensitivity to the patient's needs and the therapist's awareness of the importance of maintaining high levels of professional standards for treatment.

Voluntary Hospitalization

After careful consideration of the case and, hopefully, consultation from an experienced supervisor or colleague, hospitalization can be approached in two ways. First, consider whether voluntary hospitalization is appropriate and/or available. Is a voluntary psychiatric unit available that would accept a patient with suicide risk? Does the hospital offer appropriate forms of supervision in crisis management to minimize the risk of suicide while hospitalized? Closed doors and 24-hour suicide precautions should be available. If such a voluntary facility is available, does the client have the financial ability to seek voluntary admission? Furthermore, is the client adequately motivated to seek voluntary admission and to cooperate in inpatient treatment. In crisis, many suicidal clients may act acquiescently to a voluntary admission to reduce the chances of being involuntarily committed. However, once voluntarily admitted, many patients have left against medical advice and ultimately fulfilled the suicidal plans. The therapist must evaluate the appropriateness of a voluntary hospitalization and motivation of the client to remain in the hospital to receive the needed care and treatment.

Involuntary Hospitalization

If voluntary hospitalization is not appropriate, then the therapist should initiate civil commitments under the state's mental health statutes. Unfortunately, this decision may create serious complications between the therapist and patient. The patient may resent the perceived violation of trust and confidentiality that had existed in therapy and thus undermined future treatment. Furthermore, the therapist may be ambivalent about the necessity of commitment. These are important issues but not more important than acting to protect the client from self-harm or death. If the involuntarily committed patient does not want to continue in treatment because of the therapist's role in commitment, at least the patient will still be alive to exercise that right. The patient can always get another therapist, but a dead patient has no more options.

Civil commitment procedures and criteria vary from state to state under state law. However, there are generally accepted procedures that have evolved from the Supreme Court rulings in *Addington v. Texas* (1979) and *O'Connor v. Donaldson* (1975). These cases established dangerousness as one criterion for civil commitment. Furthermore, the Supreme Court in *Addington v. Texas* ruled that civil commitment requires a burden of proof as clear and convincing evidence (approximately 75% certainty) before a person can be involuntarily committed to a psychiatric facility against his or her wishes.

The legal concept of least restrictive alternative has evolved from a case law, which means that in theory clients should be treated in a facility with the fewest restrictions of liberty possible (*Wyatt v. Stickney* 1971). Recently, state courts have recognized the right of involuntarily committed patients to refuse some types of psychiatric care if they are not in an emergency situation (*Rennie v. Klein*, 1979 and *Rogers v. Okin* 1979). Rights to refuse treatment present new challenges to the psychiatric community.

The criteria for civil commitment require at least two separate determinations. First, the person subject to involuntary commitment must demonstrate some type of mental disorder or defect that is a diagnosable psychiatric condition. The definition of the mental disorder or defect varies from state to state and is not necessarily synonymous with DSM-III-R criteria. However, the first finding in all states for involuntary commitment is that the person be mentally disordered or defective (Miller, 1985).

The second major requirement in almost all states is the presence of dangerousness. Dangerousness, unlike a mental disorder, is not a psychiatric condition and is not the unique domain of mental health professionals. As previously summarized, our ability to predict dangerousness is very limited (Pokorny, 1983). However, the civil commitment legislation usually requires a finding as to whether the person is dangerous to him or herself or others. In some states this requires the identification of a recent overt act and not just an inferred state of dangerousness based on test data or speculation.

In civil commitment proceedings the exact diagnosis of a patient is seldom debated. However, the degree of dangerousness is often the central legal concern. In attempting to civilly commit a suicidal patient, the mental health professional should be ready to fully explain and document the reasons for feeling that this person is dangerous to her or himself or others at this point in time.

Admissions Procedures

The procedure for hospital admission varies from state to state. Generally there are two types of procedures: regular and emergency. Civil commitment is not a criminal proceeding but states do require that the person be represented by council and that due process rights are afforded, such as the right to challenge evidence against him or her and the right to counsel. The increase in legal rights began after the Supreme Court ruled 1967 in the juvenile case of *In re Gault* (1967) that due process protection should be available whenever a person's liberty is at stake, even through a civil process.

Commitment usually begins with a petitioner who initiates the civil commitment proceeding by presenting observations that allege the person meets the criteria for civil commitment: the presence of mental illness and dangerousness. An official such as a judge or magistrate then rules on the merit of the petition. If the petition is viewed as appropriate, a custody warrant is issued and the person is apprehended and required to submit to an evaluation by one or more mental health professionals. If the evaluator(s) finds that the state criteria for civil commitment is met, the person is hospitalized until a probable cause hearing is conducted in which full due process rights are available. This formal hearing occurs from 2 to 10 days following the initial evaluation and hospitalization. At this hearing the patient is represented by counsel and has the right to cross-examine witnesses and to present witnesses. If the judge or judicial officer rules that the criteria for civil commitment are met, then the patient is involuntarily hospitalized for a period varying from 2 weeks to 6 months, depending on the state. This initial period of commitment is renewable after periodic review. Once hospitalized, patients are often discharged before their completion of the commitment period. However, if their condition does not improve and recommitment is considered necessary, the state must again prove that the person meets the criteria for a civil commitment at a new hearing.

In the case of clients who are imminently suicidal, civil commitment provides a way to ensure that the client receives inpatient psychiatric care for a time-limited period during which the crisis can be addressed. Unlike 30 years ago, civil commitment is no longer a potential life sentence in a mental hospital such as portrayed in Kesey's *One Flew Over the Cuckoo's Nest* (1962).

The mental health professional should be familiar with the criteria and procedures for a civil commitment in his or her state. Most people who attempt suicide never attempt it again. Therefore, providing a potentially suicidal person with immediate care, treatment, and safety, regardless of the perceived stigma of hospitalization, may help the person cope with the acute crisis successfully and permit him or her to enjoy the remainder of life. Involuntary hospitalization, while the least preferred way of working with a client, is still a necessary part of a continuum of services when the person is unable to cope with the crisis leading to the risk of suicide.

SUMMARY

The assessment of suicide risk is a complex and multifaceted decision. It requires evaluation of demographic factors, situational-psychological indicators, direct clinical indicators, and self-report measures before an informed assessment about the degree of current suicide risk is possible. Dangerousness can be conceptualized along six dimensions: imminence of danger, target of danger, clarity of danger, intent of behavior, lethality of behavior, and probability of behavior. Depending on the careful assessment of these dimensions of dangerousness, the mental health professional has several options, ranging from continued outpatient treatment to involuntary civil commitment. There is no absolutely right or wrong treatment option. A therapist must weigh the risks and benefits of each option and consider the interaction of the client, current environment, and opportunities for self-harm and help as available in each setting. The only absolute rule for therapists is to exercise careful judgment and to carefully document the reasons for whatever decisions are reached. Consultation with a colleague is highly advisable in difficult and complex cases involving the management of a potentially suicidal client.

Whatever the outcome of the current suicidal assessment, remember that it is a time-limited assessment that is rendered at one point in time under one set of factors and circumstances. The therapist must continue to reassess the client's risk by gathering new information, and to redocument and revise treatment decisions that reflect the change in the client's situation.

Chapter 8
Strategies for Helping Suicidal Clients, Part 1: Crisis Management

According to recent surveys, suicidal clients constitute the single most stressful aspect of most therapists' work (Deutsch, 1984; Farber, 1983). In this chapter, we will present some basic principles on the management and treatment of suicidal individuals. While following these principles carries no guarantees against client suicide, risk can be lowered by recognizing differences between suicidal and nonsuicidal clients and using strategies that tailor treatment to the different kinds of suicidal individuals.

We encourage clinicians treating suicidal persons to make a distinction that is often overlooked in the literature: that between crisis management and psychotherapy. By far the bulk of material written in this area has been on "management of the suicidal client"; that is, preventing the person in crisis from committing suicide until the crisis has passed. Once the client has been stabilized and equilibrium restored, it is generally assumed that therapy will be resumed as with any other client, whether the diagnosis is depression, borderline personality, or some other disorder.

This approach presents several problems. First, it is lacking in provisions to lower the probability of future suicidal crises, so there is little assurance that the next upset will not precipitate another suicidal episode. This problem is most evident when therapy focuses on one problem after another (relationships, finances, career concerns, etc.) with-

Portions of Chapters 8 and 9 appeared previously in *Innovations in Clinical Practice* (Vol. 6) (Ellis, 1987).

out addressing the fundamental issues of the suicide option, the client's problem-solving style, or critical cognitive distortions. The client often does well until a new problem or blow to self-esteem occurs and triggers a new suicidal episode. The "flow" of therapy may be interrupted repeatedly by suicidal crises that vary in content but exhibit a similar or identical process.

Second, and relatedly, the "therapy as usual" approach fails to take into account the fact that being suicidal is not an entirely transient phenomenon; it has both state and traitlike characteristics. People who become suicidal generally differ in substantial ways from those who, although sharing the same psychiatric diagnosis, do not become suicidal. We know this both from clinical experience (e.g., many people become severely depressed, but never suicidal) and from research (to be discussed later). If these distinctions are not recognized, fit between the therapeutic approach and the client's needs may be compromised.

Finally, when the issue of suicide is dropped after the crisis has passed, the implicit message may be to communicate to the client that one's beliefs about the option of suicide is not a germane therapy issue, except during a suicidal crisis. Thus, an opportunity to effect lasting change in the client's ideas about life and death may be missed.

This is not meant to imply, however, that crisis intervention is unimportant. As Mintz (1971) pithily states, "No form of treatment is effective with a dead patient" (p. 61). Therefore, our discussion of treating the suicidal client is presented in two parts. In this chapter, we focus on interventions for minimizing suicide risk during a crisis. In Chapter 10, we turn to strategies for addressing more enduring cognitive and behavioral patterns of suicidal individuals.

CRISIS MANAGEMENT

Whether counseling college students or treating psychiatric inpatients, most therapists can expect to encounter clients in a suicidal crisis from time to time. The therapist may become aware of suicide risk during an initial assessment interview or in less opportune circumstances, such as through a distressed client's late night or weekend phone call. At such times, one must know with minimal hesitation what procedures to follow to minimize the risk of the client's injury or death through suicidal behavior.

Although few studies have been conducted to test what crisis intervention strategies most effectively reduce suicide risk, considerable agreement is found among various authorities on the subject. What follows samples from a variety of such sources, including the authors' experience. These fall under the broad headings of "therapeutic activism," delaying impulses, restoring hope, environmental intervention, and hospitalization.

Therapeutic Activism

Perhaps the point of greatest agreement among clinicians writing on this subject, from behaviorists to psychoanalysts, is the rule that during a suicidal crisis the therapist increases his or her level of activity compared with therapy during noncrisis periods (e.g., Beebe, 1975). The state of being suicidal is interpreted as an indication that the client is at present unable to engage in constructive coping, and the therapist moves to fill the void (Lesse, [1975] referred to this as an "ego transfusion"). The therapist becomes more directive and less concerned that he or she might be solving problems for the client or encouraging dependency. Therapy process issues are temporarily relegated to secondary status; the overriding goal becomes the preservation of life.

Availability becomes crucial; therapy sessions are scheduled more frequently and the therapist may instruct the client to call at designated times between sessions or may make calls him or herself. Coverage by another therapist or an agency must be arranged for periods when the primary therapist will be unavailable, even if only for a brief time. The client should be given explicit contingency plans, such as calling a telephone hotline or visiting a hospital emergency room, in the event that the primary plan fails. A "crisis card" with the phone numbers of these various resources might be provided. An individual in a suicidal crisis has a low tolerance for frustration; fruitless efforts to obtain help can be interpreted as rejection or proof that the situation is hopeless, and this can increase the probability of self-destructive acts.

Delaying Impulses

While some suicides are strategically planned over long time periods, most suicidal acts are more toward the impulsive end of the spectrum and occur in response to some acute, transient stressor or stressors. This principle is reflected in the popular adage, "Suicide is a permanent solution to a temporary problem." Accordingly, delaying the suicidal impulse becomes the immediate goal of suicidal crisis intervention. The clinician assumes that the client's communication of suicidal thoughts implies at least some desire to go on living and perhaps be rescued from simultaneous wishes to die.

Methods for delaying suicidal impulses are many and are limited only by the therapist's resourcefulness. The therapist can impress upon the client that the decision to end one's life is a serious one that must be thoroughly weighed because it cannot be reversed. The client can be reminded that suicide will always be an option later and that he or she has nothing to lose by putting it off for the time being while therapist and client work on ways to solve the immediate problems that are fueling the crisis. A firm and repeated message should be that, despite feelings to the contrary, the client can stand his or her current emotional distress, painful though it may be. The client might be asked to recall times in the past when he or she has "toughed it out." At this point, the therapist should ask the client about his or her sense of self-control and confidence in the ability to delay impulses. If the client reports feeling out of control and does not have sufficient social supports (such as family members) to serve as external controls, hospitalization should be seriously considered.

The no-suicide contract is a popular tool in many therapists' arsenals, although some disagreement exists as to its pros and cons. Certainly, it would be difficult to prove that a contract had ever kept anyone from killing him or herself. The issue of whose interests are being served—the client's or the therapist's—is pertinent here as well. However, when used properly (i.e., as a clinical intervention rather than for legal protection), it can be an effective way of both evaluating the client's current intent and sense of control and as a way of helping the client give him or herself time to work out some problems.

The agreement can be verbal or written (the latter might have more impact; if it is used, however, legalistic language should be minimized). A specific time frame should be stated and the contract should be updated as the time frame expires (Linehan, 1981). In addition to the agreement not to commit suicide during the specified time period, the contract might also list preferable options to suicide and contingency plans (such as the agreement to call the therapist when impulses become intense and to call a crisis hotline if the therapist cannot be reached). Chart 8.1 shows a sample antisuicide agreement.

Restoring Hope

Some suicidal clients may resist suggestions to delay current suicidal impulses because they see no prospect for things to improve in the future. Indeed, studies consistently have shown that a negative view of the future—hopelessness—is an important predictor of the subset of depressed people who eventually will commit suicide (e.g., Beck, Brown, & Steer, 1989). Therefore, restoration of hope can be seen as both a means of delaying impulses and as a longer term goal in the treatment of people with suicidal tendencies (Ellis, 1986).

One very effective way of combatting hopelessness has already been

Chart 8.1. Antisuicide Contract

As part of my therapy program, I, _____, agree to the follow-
                                        (name)
ing terms:

1. I agree that one of my major therapy goals is to live a long life with more pleasure and less unhappiness than I now have.

2. I understand that becoming suicidal when depressed or upset stands in the way of achieving this goal, and I therefore would like to overcome this tendency. I agree to use my therapy to learn better ways to reduce my emotional distress.

3. Since I understand that this will take time, I agree in the meantime to refuse to act on urges to injure or kill myself between this day and _____.
                                                  (date)

4. If at any time I should feel unable to resist suicidal impulses, I agree to call
_____ at _____ or _____. If this person is
        (name)   (number)   (number)
unavailable, I agree to call _____ at _____ or go
                                  (name)   (number)
directly to _____ at _____.
         (hospital or agency)   (address)

5. My therapist, _____, agrees to work with me in scheduled sessions to help me to learn constructive alternatives to self-harm and to be available as much as is reasonable during times of crisis.

6. I agree to abide by this agreement either until it expires or until it is openly renegotiated with my therapist. I understand that it is renewable at or near the expiration date of _____.
                              (date)

_____   _____
          Signature   Date

_____   _____
    Therapist's Signature   Date

---

discussed; that is, active, directive intervention by the therapist. Here, the therapist is instilling hope by communicating his or her commitment to do what is necessary to help the client through a difficult period. Ultimately, however, the central aspect of treating hopelessness lies in the client's becoming convinced that problems are solvable. Modeling of systematic problem-solving by the therapist can be one of the most effective means of getting this message across. In particular, clients who are feeling overwhelmed by multiple problems in living can be shown how identifying and addressing problems individually can improve generation of solutions and decrease feelings of hopelessness. Problem-solving training and other, more long-term approaches to dealing with the client's tendency to become hopeless are discussed in more depth in Chapter 9.

Environmental Intervention

A stance of therapeutic activism requires that the therapist's focus not be limited to the client alone. Just as the client's environment contributes to the crisis, so too can it be used as a resource for crisis resolution. The following guidelines can be used to extend the reach of therapy beyond the therapist's office walls.

Remove any easily accessible means of committing suicide, such as firearms and drugs. This may be the most immediate and practical method of preventing suicidal behavior. Firearms in particular provide a quick and lethal means of acting on suicidal impulses and account for most completed suicides in the United States. Inquiry about the availability of weapons and/or potentially lethal drugs is an essential part of the assessment of the suicidal client. When such means are available, the therapist must make every effort with the client and his or her family to remove them from the client's environment.

Involve family members and facilitate development of a network of supportive persons and/or agencies. The therapist working with a suicidal person must carefully guard against becoming the client's sole source of support. Such an arrangement carries dangers to both members of the relationship; the client is placing his or her life in only one person's hands and the therapist is taking on responsibility for a person's life (and potentially that person's death). The therapist's task is to facilitate reduction of the stressors that precipitated the crisis and to help develop multiple sources of support.

Involvement of family members sometimes requires considerable discretion on the part of the therapist. While making family members a part of treatment is a relatively straightforward (and often welcome) process for most clients, others sometimes mightily resist the idea. In these cases, the therapist must use sound judgment to determine which of the client's objections are valid and which are not. Many clients, for example, are ashamed of their emotional distress and fear that significant others may hold them in lower esteem if they learn the client's "secret." In other cases, clients may fear worrying others or may not consider themselves worth the trouble caused to others by communicating their distress. In these instances, assessing beliefs for validity and correcting mistaken ideas may not only assist in the immediate crisis but can result in considerable therapeutic benefit as well. Clients are often surprised by the supportive responses they receive when significant others learn of the severity of their distress.

Occasionally, however, the therapist must make an exception to this general rule. The case of a woman who has not told her abusive husband that she is in therapy for fear of further abuse is one example. Another example would be a case in which the therapist has observed family interactions to be so destructive that their involvement might do more harm than good. Such cases do not obviate the need for involvement of others in treatment, but rather requires that the therapist look elsewhere (e.g., to support groups or members of the clergy) for sources of support.

Make use of community resources (e.g., police, paramedics, crisis hot lines) during the acute stages of a crisis. An acute suicidal crisis often comes to the attention of a therapist through a phone call from the client and may call for immediate action by the therapist. The therapist's first step should be to determine the client's location, in case the client should lose consciousness from a drug overdose during the conversation. The phone number should also be obtained in case the client hangs up or the therapist needs to break the connection to contact others. If the client expresses intentions to commit suicide, has the means to do so, is alone, and refuses to come in for treatment, an emergency response may be required. If a home visit by the therapist is impossible or considered inappropriate, police should be apprised of the situation and asked to intervene. If the client has already injured him or herself, an ambulance must be called immediately.

Contact the client's physician regarding the potential for overdoses on prescription medications. Linehan (1981) cites studies showing that 75% to 80% of physicians treating patients who later commit suicide prescribe psychotropic drugs, and in one study prescribed medications were the cause of death in 54% of the physicians' cases (p. 278). This underscores the importance of an interdisciplinary approach to treatment.

Assist in the resolution of acute conflicts with significant others. As noted elsewhere, suicidal crises often arise from a failure to successfully resolve immediate problems. Indeed, suicidal threats and behaviors often can be seen as desperate attempts to solve these problems. Such problems are frequently interpersonal in nature and may range from a teenager's disagreement with parents over dating to marital difficulties stemming from a spouse's infidelity. A therapist's assistance in defining problems, articulating feelings, communicating wishes, and engineering solutions can prove invaluable in helping resolve stressful interpersonal conflicts. Most importantly (and this should be pointed out by the therapist), the process demonstrates the superiority of this form of problem-solving over suicidal behavior.

Help the client to structure time between therapy sessions. Because most problems will not be resolved by one therapy session or phone contact, it may be helpful to ask the client about his or her plans for the next 24 hours or few days and to offer assistance in planning activities. Depressed people in particular may suffer from a lack of enjoyable activities; the reader may wish to consult Beck, Kovacs, and Weissman (1979) for ways to evaluate and enhance a client's activity level. Aside from its antidepressant effects, structuring time can also provide a diversion from interpersonal conflict or upsetting rumination. During acute crises, the therapist should seek agreement from supportive family members or friends to stay with the client until the crisis has been resolved.

Engage in ongoing consultation with a supervisor or colleague. The therapist should solicit external support not only for the client but for him or herself as well. A trusted consultant can be used as a sounding board for understanding a client, for reality testing regarding treatment plans, or for emotional support during the crisis. If a client should commit suicide having another therapist involved can help with one's emotional reaction to the loss, as well as show that the therapist made every effort to make accurate assessments and provide optimal care for the client.

Hospitalization

When the therapist is concerned about imminent danger because the client may not delay impulses or the client's environment cannot provide sufficient support, hospitalization should be considered. While far from being a long-range remedy for suicidal behavior, hospitalization can provide several distinct benefits, including (a) external structure to assist with impulse control, (b) temporary respite from family conflict and other sources of life stress, (c) time and resources to develop alternate problem-solving strategies, (d) reduction in self-abasement through exposure to other people with similar problems, and (e) opportunity to receive medical treatments such as medications or electroconvulsive therapy. In addition, hospitalization communicates to significant others the seriousness of the client's distress and often results in rallying of support systems.

To use hospitalization wisely, the therapist must be aware also of its drawbacks and potential misuses. No less than a therapeutic drug, hospitalization carries with it undesirable side effects. It may, for instance, inadvertently reinforce suicidal behavior as a means of effecting change or eliciting support unless this issue is explicitly addressed during treatment. Additionally (especially in repeat attempters), hasty hospitalization may imply to the client that he or she is incapable of controlling impulses and must rely upon some other person or persons to survive a crisis.

Finally, in the modern-day climate of fear of litigation, many therapists feel pressured to hospitalize as a means of legal risk reduction. Just as the same type of pressure may push obstetricians toward unnecessary Caesarian sections, so too do some therapists hospitalize questionably suicidal clients for fear of being sued by angry relatives should the client commit suicide. From an empirical standpoint, this is less likely than many might assume. For example, the chances of a psychologist's being sued is about one half of one percent per year; of these, only about 9% of cases were brought for wrongful death, or suicide (Turkington, 1986). As discussed elsewhere in this book, making one's best clinical judgment under the circumstances and engaging in appropriate procedures such as keeping accurate records and consulting colleagues may be the most effective approach to minimizing legal liability.

From a clinical standpoint, any lowered risk to the therapist must be viewed against possible antitherapeutic effects of the treatment, especially involuntary hospitalization. As observed by Hendin (1982), the therapist must guard against making the patient's survival a battle of wills.

> Since many suicidal patients are themselves preoccupied with management and control, therapy can become a contest in which the suicidal patient usually obtains his or her pills if he or she really wants them and in which the therapist is reassured that all possible precautions have been taken . . . [This] may result in encouraging one of the most lethal aspects of the suicidal individual, that is, his tendency to make someone else responsible for his staying alive. . . . The best chance for helping the patient lies in understanding and helping him with the problems that are making him suicidal, including most specifically the way in which he uses the threat of death. (p. 160–162)

Linehan (1981) expresses a similar view:

> The focus of intervention [may] slip from concentration on remedying problems functionally related to the suicidal behavior to a more exclusive concentration on preventing the suicidal behaviors in the short run. . . . [S]uch short run considerations may be inimical to the long-term interests of patients. Additionally, communication to the patient that the therapist has assumed final responsibility for the patient's behavior may lead to counter-control problems in which the patient believes that freedom of choice has been lost. (pp. 276–277)

Obviously, no simple formula for hospitalization exists; the therapist can only become familiar with its advantages and disadvantages and strive to focus on what is in the client's best interest, both in the short run and long-term. Our best advice is to follow a model of collaborative therapy (Beck et al., 1979), in which the aims of therapy are mutually agreed on and conflict between client and therapist is minimized because both are working toward commonly shared goals.

Chapter 9
Strategies for Helping Suicidal Clients, Part 2: Therapy

Recent years have seen a few attempts to improve therapy with suicidal clients by developing procedures specifically designed for them (e.g., Clum, Patsiokas, & Luscomb, 1979; Linehan, 1981; Patsiokas & Clum, 1985; Ellis, 1986). Table 9.1 lists suggestions by Linehan (1981) that represent sound general therapeutic procedures for suicidal clients. Her chapter is recommended for the reader desiring further details on these guidelines. In the following section, we will present a rationale and procedures for a cognitively oriented therapy for the suicidal client. Cognitive forms of therapy have been shown to be highly effective with a number of disorders and show promise for equally effective application to suicidal phenomena.

Before proceeding, let us preface any therapy recommendations with a comment about the varieties of suicide. While many treatment guides refer to suicide generically, we prefer to view it as a multidimensional phenomenon. Suicide might be likened to cancer or headaches, either of which can have a variety of etiologies and symptom clusters. The mere existence or possibility of a final common pathway (self-inflicted death) cannot be assumed to indicate either a common cause or identical treatment.

For example, attempted suicide (parasuicide) is often assumed to be a nonfatal variant of completed suicide, with the two existing on a continuum of severity. As discussed in Chapter 3, however, epidemiological data show important differences between these two groups on such variables as age, gender, and method of self-harm. Clinical experience also reveals differences in diagnostic makeup and motivational fac-

Table 9.1. Guidelines for Treating Suicidal Clients

General Procedures

1. Talk about suicide openly and matter-of-factly.
2. Avoid perjorative explanations of suicidal behavior or motives.
3. Present a problem-solving theory of suicidal behavior, and maintain the stance that suicide is a maladaptive and/or ineffective solution.
4. Involve significant others, including other therapists.
5. Schedule sessions frequently enough, and maintain session discipline such that at least some therapy time is devoted to long-term treatment goals.
6. Stay aware of the multitude of variables impinging on patients, and avoid omnipotent taking or accepting of responsibility for patient's suicidal behaviors.
7. Maintain professional consultation with a colleague.
8. Maintain occasional contact with persons who reject therapy.

Precrisis Planning Procedures

9. Anticipate and plan for crisis situations.
10. Continually assess the risk of suicide and parasuicide.
11. Be accessible.
12. Use local emergency/crisis/suicide services.
13. Give the patient a crisis card: telephone numbers of therapist, police, emergency, hospital, significant others.
14. Keep telephone numbers and addresses of patients and their significant others with you.
15. Make a short-term antisuicide contract, and keep it up to date.
16. Contact the patient's physician regarding the risks of overprescribing medications.

Therapeutic Maintenance Procedures

17. Do not force the patient to resort to suicidal talk or ideation in order to get your attention.
18. Express your caring openly; provide noncontingent warmth and attention.
19. Clarify and reinforce nonsuicidal responses to problems.
20. Identify to the patient likely therapist responses to the patient's suicidal behaviors (e.g., if the patient dies, the therapist will be sad, but will continue on with life).
21. Ensure that the patient has realistic expectations about the responses of others to future suicidal behaviors.

Source. H. Glazer and J. Clarkin (Eds.), *Depression: Behavioral and directive intervention strategies* (pp. 229–294) by M. Linehan, 1981, New York: Garland. Copyright 1981 by Garland.

tors. Although most discussions of suicide focus on persons with major depression, suicide is associated with a variety of clinical syndromes. We might include the following in a list of "types" of suidical persons:

Depressed/hopeless
Communication/control
Psychotic
Alcoholic
Organic brain dysfunction
"Rational" suicide
Mixed type

A different "push" toward suicidal behavior might be posited for each type, thereby suggesting a somewhat different treatment approach. Each type will now be discussed in turn.

Depression is clearly the most common syndrome associated with completed suicide, accounting for up to 80% of self-inflicted death (Murphy, 1985). The lifetime risk of suicide for depressed individuals is 15%. While this is substantial, it is important to note that the vast majority of depressed persons do not commit suicide. Studies (e.g., Minkoff, Bergman, Beck, & Beck, 1973) have shown that a critical connection between depression and suicide is hopelessness. Other variables distinguishing between depressed persons who do and do not become suicidal are discussed in a later section.

The depressed/hopeless person's motive to suicidal behavior is cessation of life. This individual has lost hope of achieving relief from his or her suffering by any means other than death, and is therefore unlikely to attempt suicide as a "cry for help." Attempts are generally of high lethality (e.g., gunshot or jumping) and planned rather than impulsive. Survival is often greeted with disappointment rather than relief.

The communication/control picture is quite different. More likely to be associated with personality disorder than major affective disorder, suicidal behavior in this individual frequently takes the form of low lethality attempts or suicide threats. Motivation behind attempting suicide is related to a desire to effect situational changes, most often of an interpersonal nature. These individuals often readily acknowledge that they did not desire to die, but could think of no other way to "get his attention" or "show how much I was hurting." Attempts are generally impulsive, and psychological functioning is often seen to improve dramatically following hospital admission. This form of suicidal behavior is certainly not to be dismissed lightly, however. A substantial number of these individuals eventually die as a result of suicidal behavior, and previous parasuicidal behavior remains one of the best predictors of completed suicide.

Psychosis, whether secondary to affective disorder or schizophrenia, presents a major risk for suicide. Schizophrenics are at similar risk for suicide to depressed patients, with a 10% to 12% lifetime risk. In a study of 134 completed suicides (Robins, 1986), 19% were found to have been psychotic at the time of their deaths. Here, the push to suicide is often in the form of delusions or command hallucinations, in which the patient feels, not so much a wish, but a compulsion to die. However, it is also not unusual (and may be more the rule) that persons with these major psychiatric disorders commit suicide during a period of remission when they become despondent over the damage done to their lives by their illness.

It is surprising to many to learn that more than one in five persons who die by suicide are alcoholic (Murphy, 1985). Suicide often follows alcohol-related losses such as being divorced or fired from one's job. Additionally, alcoholism often coexists with other disorders. In cases of depression, for example, intoxication may comingle with hopelessness in such a way as to produce the disinhibition needed to pull a trigger or drive into a bridge abutment.

Organic brain dysfunction also presents risk for suicide. The conglomerate of organic problems, including head injury, cerebrovascular accident (stroke), and epilepsy, among others, account for 5% to 10% of completed suicides (Murphy, 1985). Causal mechanisms are not well understood, and range from psychodynamic theories of ego regression (Rice, 1973), to theories of behavioral aberrations due to organically based hallucinations and delusions, to affective disorders precipitated by traumatically induced biochemical disturbances (Whitlock, 1982). Indeed, some evidence suggests that subclinical neuropsychological dysfunction might account for some of the cognitive characteristics (such as cognitive rigidity, discussed below) found in suicidal patients without known brain pathology (Ellis, Berg, and Franzen, 1989). Certainly, dealing with the organically impaired patient requires a multidisciplinary effort to deal with suicidal tendencies attributable both to the primary organic disorder and to the patient's reaction to his loss of cognitive capacity.

"Rational" suicide is a matter that involves both philosophical and empirical issues, and cannot be discussed fully here. In hearing about the profound troubles of some clients (e.g., catastrophic family losses or severe physical maladies), clinicians sometimes feel that suicidal impulses are "understandable under the circumstances" and do not constitute irrational or disordered functioning. Treatment of such individuals can therefore be perplexing, due to the clinician's desire to respect individual values and hesitance to broach profound philosophical issues. On the other hand, it should be noted that most people, even in extremely difficult circumstances, do not become suicidal; those who do are probably suffering from some form of psychological impairment. This is an empirical question that has not as yet been thoroughly researched. One study that did address the issue (Brown et al., 1986) found that of 44 terminally ill cancer patients, only 3 had considered suicide, and all 3 were suffering from major depression. Obviously, the clinician is well advised to thoroughly assess for psychological disturbance, regardless of circumstances.

It must be emphasized that no empirical validity is claimed for the "typology" described above. It is offered primarily as a device to outline dimensions to consider in treating suicidal individuals. It seems reasonable to expect that most suicidal persons would fall into two or more overlapping categories (e.g., depressed and psychotic or alcoholic and communication/control) rather than representing "pure" types. This is another area of suicidal behavior that has yet to be thoroughly researched. (For an overview of the literature and discussion of issues involved in suicide typology, the reader is referred to Ellis, 1988.)

OVERVIEW OF COGNITIVE THERAPY

Cognitive therapy has become such a force in the treatment of emotional and behavioral disorders that it hardly needs a lengthy exposition here. Briefly, the term refers to a collection of similar therapeutic approaches developed by several theorists (e.g., Ellis & Dryden, 1987; Beck, Rush, Shaw, & Emery, 1979; Meichenbaum, 1977). While having some significant differences, they maintain as their central tenet the view that psychological disorders are in large part attributable to idiosyncrasies in the way an individual processes experience. Theorized anomalies range from Seligman's depressive explanations for bad events (Peterson & Seligman, 1984) to Ellis's irrational beliefs (Ellis, 1962), and Beck's cognitive distortions and negative schemas (Beck, Rush, Shaw, & Emery, 1979).

Several basic hypotheses make up the common threads tying cognitive theories together. First, cognitions are thought to exist in a causal relationship to human behavior and affective experience. Though not claimed to be the sole source of emotions, cognitions are thought to be a major influence in an individual's emotional reactions to internal and external events. For example, studies have shown that consistently blaming oneself for things that go wrong heightens risk for depression and that believing that one must perform perfectly well and please others contributes to the development of performance anxiety.

A second hypothesis is that these faulty cognitions are relatively *accessible and modifiable*. While such cognitive processes are generally beyond the awareness of the individual before therapy, they can be brought to awareness through several straightforward procedures, such as monitoring and recording thoughts regarding stressful situations. Modifications are made through a variety of techniques, including showing the errors in various beliefs and attitudes, teaching self-statements containing more adaptive ideas, and providing behavioral homework assignments that help develop and reinforce cognitions and behaviors more conducive to emotional well-being.

A third hypothesis, following from the first two, is that correcting faulty cognitions will lead to corresponding improvements in associated target symptoms. A considerable amount of literature has accumulated that provides support for this hypothesis (e.g., DiGiuseppe & Miller, 1977; Peterson & Seligman, 1984; Simons, Murphy, Levine, & Wetzel, 1986).

A number of authors have described attempts to tailor cognitive therapy to specific disorders. Best known is Beck and colleagues' thorough description of depression and development of a structured, time-limited cognitive therapy (Beck, Rush, Shaw, & Emery, 1979). More recently, Beck has produced an equally thorough description of cognitive therapy for anxiety disorders (Beck & Emery, 1985). We also have seen cognitive therapies developed for anger problems (Novaco, 1977), eating disorders (Garner, 1986), stress disorders (Meichenbaum & Jaremko, 1983), chronic pain (Turk, Meichenbaum, & Genest, 1983), and insomnia (Borkovec, 1982). We propose that this principle of treatment specificity might also be applied to the suicidal client.

UNIQUE CHARACTERISTICS OF SUICIDAL INDIVIDUALS

Before one can justify a treatment tailor made for a specific disorder, it first must be shown that clients with that disorder are sufficiently different from other clients to warrant a distinct treatment. Several lines of evidence show that suicidal individuals differ from others in areas of direct relevance to the practice of cognitive therapy. These findings are especially interesting in light of the difficulty distinguishing the suicidal person on other measures, such as personality inventories (e.g., Watson, Klett, Walters, & Vassar, 1984). Only a brief overview of this literature will be presented here because more thorough reviews are available elsewhere (Neuringer, 1976; Arffa, 1983; Ellis, 1986).

Cognitive Rigidity

Suicidal people often show a remarkable inability to consider alternative possibilities to their current situations or world views. Subject to interpretation as resistance, this may be a manifestation of a genuine inability to generate alternatives, a basic component of effective problem-solving (see below).

Dichotomous Thinking

Dichotomous, or black-and-white, thinking refers to a tendency to think in polar extremes instead of shades of gray. Thus, people are either good or evil, smart or stupid, rather than a mixture of desirable and undesirable characteristics.

Impaired Problem-solving Ability

While most depressed persons have difficulty solving problems, suicidal individuals do especially poorly on problem-solving measures. This finding has been shown to extend to children and adolescents, as well as adults.

Hopelessness

Perhaps representing the culmination of cognitive rigidity, dichotomous thinking, and deficient problem-solving, hopelessness has been shown to be an important link between depression and suicidal tendencies. Minkoff et al., (1973) and others (e.g., Ellis & Ratliff, 1986) have shown hopelessness to predict suicidal thinking more reliably than severity of depression.

Irrational Beliefs and Dysfunctional Attitudes

In an attempt to learn more about sources of hopelessness, Ellis and Ratliff (1986) tested equally depressed groups of suicidal and nonsuicidal psychiatric inpatients. Specific areas of dysfunctional thinking that emerged were a marked tendency to view unhappiness as resulting from circumstances rather than one's view of them and excessive needs for success and approval. This was consistent with previous findings suggesting that suicidal persons are more likely than controls to possess an external locus of control (e.g., Williams & Nickels, 1969).

Although the research in this area is not without its share of methodological shortcomings, the aggregate of studies suggests that there are important, probably clinically significant, differences between clients who become suicidal and those who do not. In this context, the practitioner must ask whether it is appropriate to use interventions with suicidal clients that are no different from those used with other clients. What might be the interventions of choice for individuals with the particular set of cognitive characteristics manifested by suicidal persons?

THERAPY PLANNING FOR THE SUICIDAL CLIENT: A COMPONENT APPROACH

As indicated earlier in discussing the various forms of the suicide phenomenon (depressed/hopeless, control/communication, etc.), it is rather unrealistic to expect to be able to rely on a typology for individual assessment and treatment planning. Many or most clients are likely to belong to overlapping categories. An alternative is, as follows, to assess various aspects of the individual's functioning. (Linehan, 1981, is recommended to the reader as an alternative and compatible approach to analyzing suicidal behavior.)

The experienced cognitive therapist remains mindful of the fact that a person is much more than a mere collection of cognitive processes. Thus, while the guiding purpose of the therapy is to change the way the client processes experience, unless emotions and behaviors also change, cognitive change per se remains pointless. Similarly, methods changing cognitions should not be limited to cognitive interventions, but must include behavioral and affective work as well. The client's physical condition and living environment also should not be overlooked in seeking the most effective and efficient treatment strategy. To say that cognitions are important is not to say that other aspects of the person do not matter.

Effective and efficient therapy requires clear identification of therapy change targets. The following five aspects of functioning can be considered:

Affect
Behavior
Cognition
Organic conditions
Situational factors

Any or all of these might require modification in order to achieve a successful outcome. Each will be discussed in the context of the suicidal client, focusing on aspects that might be accessed in therapy and the change of which might be expected to lead to higher functioning and a lower probability of suicidal thinking and behavior. It should be noted that each component might manifest differently, depending on the "type" of suicide under consideration (for example, the primary affective state for the depressed/hopeless type is depression, while for the control/communication type it might be anger).

Affect

The primary affective state to be considered is depression. Various treatments for depression have been described (e.g., Beck, Rush, Shaw, & Emery, 1979), and may range from cognitive restructuring to behavior modification or pharmacotherapy. Other problematic emotions must be considered as well, however. Absent from many discussions of suicide is the role of anger—that is interpersonal anger, rather than the traditional "anger turned inward." Not infrequently, we deal with the patient who is threatening suicide or has made an attempt, in which the precipitating factor is a significant other with whom the client is frustrated or upset. Another emotion whose role in suicide is poorly understood is panic (cf. Pegeron & Curtis, 1986). One client, for example, although suffering from a major depressive disorder, attempted suicide only when feeling "panicked" that she might never have a lifetime companion. Work with her combined cognitive therapy concerning her fears of not being able to manage on her own with coping skills training to help her manage her panic states. While depression is easily the most common affective state associated with suicide, it is incumbent on the therapist to remain alert for other associated affective problems.

Behavioral Deficits

This component may come into play in a variety of forms. Perhaps most important is problem-solving behavior. Deficient problem-solving skills have been shown to be associated with suicide and can be expected to be linked in many cases to hopelessness. This surely must also account for many suicide attempts labelled "manipulative." Training in interpersonal problem-solving (D'Zurilla, 1986) and/or assertiveness skills (e.g., Alberti & Emmons, 1974) can provide less hazardous and less alienating goal-directed behaviors and might be expected to lower the incidence of attempts whose purpose is to influence rather than end life. Other behavioral deficits that might be targeted for various types of suicidal clients include underactivity, lack of pleasurable pursuits, and excessive alcohol consumption.

Cognitive Vulnerabilities

The primary cognitive aspect of being suicidal is hopelessness. While some might consider this more appropriately placed in the affect category, hopelessness stems from a negative cognitive appraisal of the future (Beck, Rush, Shaw, & Emery, 1979). Hopelessness often results from overgeneralizing, both in terms of a current evaluation (since some things are bad, everything is bad) and in terms of the future (because things are bad now, they always will be). We also can see how the irrational belief, mentioned earlier, that one's happiness or misery is caused by one's situation can lead one to hopelessness, because one's situation may not be likely to change soon. Other targets for cognitive change might include the entire range of irrational beliefs and cognitive distortions described by Ellis, Beck, and others. It might be particularly important to bring to the patient's attention tendencies toward rigidity and black-and-white thinking, which research has identified as risk factors for suicide.

Organic Factors

This category is so broad that an entire book had been published devoted exclusively to connections between biology and suicide (Maris, 1986). Most important for our purposes is to consider the possibility that a given client might have a biochemically based depression that would respond to an antidepressant medication. Another risk factor, organic brain dysfunction, was discussed earlier. Some evidence suggests that patients are too infrequently evaluated for cortical integrity (Ellis, Berg, & Franzen, 1989).

Situational Stresses

Although cognitive therapists emphasize that emotional distress stems largely from assessments of situations rather than from the situations themselves, this does not exclude environmental changes as a legitimate part of the therapy endeavor. This appears especially important for adolescents. At least one study (Cohen-Sandler, Berman, & King, 1982) has suggested that inescapable situational stress, perhaps more than psychological problems, is an important predictor of suicide among teenagers. Additionally, teaching clients more effective ways to produce situational changes can be a potent means of breaking a vicious failure-hopelessness cycle.

COGNITIVE THERAPY WITH THE SUICIDAL CLIENT

We now come to the question of what cognitive therapy looks like within this framework. For purposes of this discussion, we will focus on two client categories: the depressed/hopeless category, which accounts for the great majority of completed suicides, and the communication/control category, which constitutes a major portion of the suicide contemplators and nonfatal attempts seen in clinical practice.

The Depressed/Hopeless Client

In addition to the treatment suggestions outlined below, cognitive therapy with this individual includes all aspects of comprehensive cognitive therapy with any depressed client. Treatment procedures have been thoroughly described elsewhere, and include correction of faulty cognitions (such as negative prediction and overgeneralization) and restructuring of negative schemas and underlying assumptions. For complete discussions of these concepts and treatment processes, the interested reader is referred to the original descriptions (e.g., Beck, Rush, Shaw, & Emery, 1979; Wright & Beck, 1983). This discussion will focus on those characteristics that distinguish the depressed suicidal individual from clients who are depressed but not suicidal.

Hopelessness. Various authors have described strategies for dealing with hopelessness. Trexler (1973), for example, recommended supportive yet firm disputation of the client's "exaggerated and overgeneralized negative evaluations of the world, the future, and most importantly, of himself" (p. 21). Beck, Rush, Shaw, & Emery, (1979) discussed a variety of methods to show the patient that (a) there are less pessimistic ways of viewing one's life situation and (b) there are alternatives to one's current problem-producing behaviors. In addition, addressing other cognitive and behavioral liabilities, such as dichotomous thinking and ineffective problem-solving, can be expected to facilitate the development of hope.

Perhaps most important, at least initially, is communication of the therapist's optimism for the client. The effective therapist must be convinced that the client's conviction that he or she is a failure and beyond hope is indeed erroneous and that he or she will indeed experience improvement in outlook and mood once faulty cognitions are corrected. This does not in any sense require a Pollyannish attitude on the part of the therapist, but merely confidence in his or her technique and understanding of the client's tendency to think negatively and underestimate his or her capabilities. The importance of this realistic optimism is described by Frank (1973) as one of the more important antidotes for "demoralization," and is well exemplified by David Burns in his self-help book, *Feeling Good* (1980), which the therapist may wish to recommend to clients early in treatment. In addition, it is especially important to educate the client about depression, "cognitive filters," and hopelessness. Hopelessness should be labelled as a *symptom* of the client's disorder (depression combined with various cognitive distortions) and as a suicide risk factor that can be eliminated. The client can be explicitly told that "feelings are not facts" and "your feeling hopeless does not mean that your situation is hopeless—it simply means that you are depressed."

Rigidity. Client education and sensitization, used in most forms of cognitive therapy, may be especially important in dealing with the suicidal client's cognitive rigidity. Unawareness of this tendency might contribute to the client's failure to seek alternatives to his or her current perception of reality, whereas recognizing rigidity as part of a syndrome can serve as a cue for the client to question negative perceptions and evaluations rather than accept them as unquestionable facts. Treating rigidity as a target symptom can also be helpful in averting power struggles in which the client tries to save face by defending his or her viewpoint while accusing the therapist of minimizing the seriousness of matters. Encouraging an atmosphere that Beck has termed "collaborative empiricism," in which client and therapist objectively test out the client's negative world view and negative predictions, can help establish rapport as well as decrease rigidity. Finally, cognitive rigidity might be addressed through such exercises as role playing with role reversal and homework assignments designed to provide practice at generating alternatives. Guided imagery (e.g., Lazarus, 1984) might prove useful in helping such alternatives come alive.

Dichotomous thinking. Strategies for modifying black-and-white thinking have been described by Burns (1980) and Beck, Rush, Shaw, and Emery (1979), and follow a paradigm similar to procedures for correcting other cognitive errors. Episodes of emotional upset can be monitored by the client, who records precipitating events and associated automatic thoughts. Thought records are assessed during the therapy session for examples of dichotomous thinking. Client and therapist can then use insession and homework exercises designed to find gray areas between polar extremes and develop language less inclined to polarize experience (e.g., "I didn't do well on the test; French just isn't my cup of tea," rather than "Failing the test proves how stupid I am.").

Ineffective problem-solving. Whether considered alone or as a consequence of other processes (e.g., rigidity and dichotomous thinking), ineffective problem-solving must be considered as a possible target for the alleviation of hopelessness and suicidal thinking (Schotte & Clum, 1987). Suicidal people generally will acknowledge that they desire not to die, but to end their suffering, and suffering is commonly attributed to problems that seem endless, unavoidable, and insoluble. Problem-solving might be interfered with by cognitive rigidity, dichotomous thinking, lack of energy, amotivation due to depression, or simply ignorance of sound problem-solving strategies. If the latter is the case, training interventions described by Spivack, Platt, and Shure (1976) or D'Zurilla (1986) might prove helpful. They focus on improving problem identification and generating and testing potential solutions. Also emphasized is the adoption of a problem-solving "set," in which problems are viewed as a normal part of life rather than as situations that "shouldn't" exist (Ellis, 1962).

Kiev (1975) describes a program for suicidal clients applying principles of problem-solving. This program combines chemotherapy and supportive therapy with the teaching of "life strategy skills" to help patients cope with the demands of daily living. Cohen-Sandler and Berman (1982) provided training in interpersonal problem-solving to suicidal children and found significant gains in their ability to generate solutions and respond more planfully to problematic situations. Beck, Rush, Shaw, & Emery (1979) also discuss problem-solving strategies applied specifically to the suicidal patient. Patsiokas and Clum (1985) recently reported positive results from a controlled study of problem-solving training in the treatment of suicidal patients.

View of suicide as a desirable solution. Related to ineffective problem-solving, the view of suicide as a desirable solution is perhaps the most definitive feature of the depressed suicidal individual. It could well be the sine qua non of suicide. Here, it is essential that the therapist has a firm, objective grasp on the advantages and disadvantages of killing oneself. (Needless to say, it is very helpful if the therapist is thoroughly convinced that suicide would not be a good idea.) While most therapists might find it peculiar to be exploring the advantages of suicide with a suicidal client, it is essential to obtain clarification of the client's reasons for thinking that suicide is a viable alternative before any attempt at disputation or cognitive restructuring. This allows the client to feel he or she is being listened to (instead of being talked out of something) and gives the therapist access to thinking errors. Some of the more common justifications for suicide are: "I can't take the pain anymore;" "This pain will never end;" "I'm just a burden to my family and friends;" "I have no reason to go on living;" and "I just want some peace." (The reader will notice that the tone of these statements is quite different from statements such as "I can't stand to live without him or her" and "They'll be sorry when I'm gone." These would be more consistent with the communication/control client, to be discussed below.)

Statements justifying suicide usually point directly toward cognitive distortions, which then can be corrected by various means. For example, the statement, "My family would be better off without me" can be questioned by asking the client to realistically imagine his or her own suicide, becoming aware of the permanence of death and the grief that family members would experience. This exercise also challenges the implied belief that the family now receives no benefit whatever from the client's existence. The client can also be reminded that his or her depression is probably the main "burden" in question, and that once the depression is eliminated, so too will this reason for suicide.

In addition to logical disputation, clients can be asked to vividly imagine real or fabricated problematic situations and to practice generating solutions. Included in this process should be a frank assessment of the advantages and disadvantages of suicide as a solution relative to other possible solutions. Clients are often surprisingly adept at thinking of disadvantages of suicide.

External locus of control. While the empirical data is somewhat inconsistent, we do have some evidence suggesting that the clinician should assess suicidal clients for their beliefs about how their unhappiness is created and maintained. In a comparison of suicidal depressed and nonsuicidal depressed inpatients, Ellis and Ratliff (1986) found a significant difference on only 1 of 10 subscales on the Irrational Beliefs Test. Suicidal patients scored significantly higher on the tendency to believe that their emotional problems were caused by their circumstances, rather than by how they dealt with those circumstances. A natural progression from feeling at the mercy of one's situation to feeling hopeless when that situation does not change can be predicted. This highlights the importance of the educational phase of cognitive therapy for the suicidal patient. While most forms of cognitive therapy educate clients about the role that their attitudes and beliefs play in creating their problematic emotions and behaviors, it might be especially helpful to demonstrate to the suicidal client that one's emotional state can be improved by changing how one processes experience. One of many ways of demonstrating this point is to ask the client to think of examples of people coping well in difficult circumstances and to speculate how they managed to maintain their emotional well-being. This exercise almost always results in cognitive solutions, which then can provide ideas for use in the client's own life.

Other cognitive distortions. As stated earlier, the faulty cognitions specified here set the suicidal client apart from other depressed clients, but are by no means the only errors to be expected from suicidal individuals. The therapist must be alert also for a range of other cognitive

errors, such as overestimating the magnitude or insolubility of problems ("catastrophizing"), underestimating one's ability to solve problems, rating one's worth rather than one's performance, and so forth.
Techniques for modifying such maladaptive attitudes and beliefs are
described by Wright and Beck (1983) and Walen, DiGiuseppe, and
Wessler (1980).

Case example. "Randy" was a 25-year-old, white, divorced male with a
high school education, who sought therapy for his chronic depression.
Just prior to calling for an appointment, he had loaded his shotgun
and walked alone into the woods near his home with the intention of
ending his life. When asked what had stopped him from pulling the
trigger, he ruefully stated that he had not had the "guts." His developmental history included a lonely, sad childhood in a home with criticism, bickering, and minimal parental warmth or encouragement. A
prominent childhood memory was of his mother putting a towel over
the window in the front door so that visitors would not know anyone
was at home. His social history was characterized by repeated job
changes and unsatisfactory relationships. His 6-month marriage had
ended a few weeks before his suicidal episode.

Randy was preoccupied with his failures, had profound feelings of
inadequacy, and was convinced that he would "never amount to anything." He showed a strong tendency toward black-and-white thinking, as was evident in his belief that he was totally to blame for the
breakup of his marriage. This was associated with extreme cognitive
rigidity, as seen in his persistent refusal initially to entertain the idea
of mutual responsibility for the outcome of a relationship. Problem-
solving skills were much less than needed in his troubled situation;
when confronted with a stressor, he typically responded with passivity
and then berated himself for his inadequacy.

Cognitive therapy focused heavily on this latter issue, helping Randy
to articulate his current, harsh philosophy regarding human worth and
to replace it with a more compassionate attitude of acceptance of human fallibility. Thought-monitoring homework was used to great ad-
vantage in identifying self-deprecatory thinking and developing alternative self-statements such as, "It's too bad I made that mistake, but I
don't have to punish myself for it. I'll try and learn from it and do
better next time." Information was provided both verbally by the therapist and through assigned readings to give Randy a vocabulary and
framework for detecting such cognitive errors as black-and-white thinking
and "fortune telling." This was used as a springboard for learning to
find gray areas between the extremes and to resist the urge to jump to
negative conclusions. The option of suicide was discussed openly and

with the same "let's explore the advantages and disadvantages" problem-solving approach. Randy was soon able to view hopelessness as an idea rather than a fact and to recognize that killing himself would not get him what he wanted as well as other, less costly strategies.

As of this writing, the focus of therapy has shifted from issues of suicide and self-worth to social adjustment and interpersonal relationships. A recent sign of successful resolution of the suicide dilemma emerged following the end of a 3-month relationship with a woman. Though sad and tearful, Randy acknowledged that the idea of suicide had not entered his mind. When asked how he accounted for this, he replied that he did not feel blameworthy for the breakup and therefore had no reason to harm himself. Asked about his plans, he responded that he had already called a dating service and was looking forward to going out with a new acquaintance.

The Communication/Control Client

The client who threatens or attempts suicide for purposes other than cessation of life is a major source of concern for most therapists. Therapist attitudes toward this client are often a mixture of concern for the welfare of the client and irritation for their use of such a troublesome coping strategy. This latter reaction is evident in such perjorative expressions as "suicide gesture," "manipulative attempt," and "nonserious attempt." Hankoff (1979) provides a cogent description of this category of suicidal client, whom he refers to as "stress attempters." Before their suicidal episodes, these individuals often have been involved in a stressful situation marked more by their heightened emotionality than by the severity of the stressor. Psychiatric diagnoses often include a personality disorder, not uncommonly the somewhat maligned diagnosis of borderline personality. These clients are generally found to be younger and more predominantly female than depressed suicidal clients. The emotion experienced is often anger or hostility rather than depression, and attempts are generally impulsive rather than premeditated. Attempts are often of low lethality, but high lethality attempts are not uncommon. Recovery after the attempt may be dramatic, with the client disavowing any intention toward suicide days or even hours after an intervention is initiated.

These clients are often derided by hospital and mental health staff, particularly if they are known from their previous crises. They are known for late night telephone calls and emergency hospital admissions, sometimes followed by departures from the hospital against medical advice. Mental health workers often feel manipulated by this individual, who with each crisis seems more and more like the boy who cried wolf. What is often overlooked, however, is that these are all reasons to take this client more, rather than less, seriously. Clearly, these individuals are the source of considerable stress for therapists, as well as the recipients of significant mental health resources. Most importantly, estimates are that 10% of these individuals eventually kill themselves. Effective treatment would be mutually beneficial to client and system alike.

This type of client is less well described, both clinically and empirically, than the suicidal depressed client. Making things more difficult is the failure of most studies of suicidal patients to distinguish these two groups from one another. (One exception is Marsha Linehan's (1987) comprehensive "dialectical-behavioral" approach to working with this category of client.) Empirical limitations notwithstanding, clinical experience does allow a beginning, if necessarily tentative, description of a cognitive approach to treatment. As before, we will proceed by discussing, in turn, various cognitive vulnerabilities of these individuals and ways of working with them in therapy.

Suicidal behavior as an interpersonal problem-solving strategy. Unlike suicidal depression, wherein the problem is suffering and the perceived solution is death, the control/communication attempter's problem is situational and the perceived solution is leverage within a relationship through the threat of death. The relationship in question may range from one's spouse to one's therapist to a physician resisting admission of the client to the hospital. In describing this subsample in his study, Hankoff (1979) stated that this client saw his suicidal behavior as "an entirely appropriate reaction" and that a suicide attempt was "a normal solution or tactic in the course of an interpersonal exchange" (p. 245).

Rather than judging these individuals for their bothersome behavior, it is essential that the clinician ask how it is that one would choose such a desperate, stigmatizing behavior to achieve a desired outcome in a relationship. One reason, of course, is that it works. Suicidal behavior tends to elicit immediate attention and caring, at least from the service system, if not from significant others as well. This no doubt accounts for much of the rapid improvement in the clinical picture of these patients after admission to an inpatient setting.

However, perhaps a more constructive consideration would be to ask why this person had to resort to such extreme behavior in the first place. Two possibilities can be hypothesized: (a) unresponsiveness on the part of the significant other and (b) the client's inadequate repertoire of problem-solving strategies. Certainly it is possible to target the former for change, such as through family therapy (especially if the client is a child or adolescent). However, this must not deter the practitioner from attending to deficient problem-solving skills as perhaps the preeminent problem, for not all people with unresponsive families resort to desperate, self-harmful behavior.

Addressing suicide as maladaptive problem-solving might be approached as a three-stage process. Before training in effective problem-solving strategies can take place, the client must first become aware of the goal-oriented nature of his or her behavior. Contrary to labeling suicide threats or attempts as "manipulation," the therapist might frame the behavior as what people do when they see no other ways to fulfill their desires ("desires" is preferable to "needs" for reasons which will become clear later). In this manner, the therapist makes it clear that no value judgment is being passed and the client will be in a better position to nondefensively move to the second stage of intervention, namely, examining the various advantages and disadvantages of suicidal behavior and exploring alternative ways of getting what one wants. In the third stage of intervention, the client is taught how to clearly identify the problem, generate possible solutions, select the most advantageous strategies, and implement, evaluate, and modify solutions (D'Zurilla, 1986).

Excessive affect. As stated above, the communication/control client shows a strong tendency toward reacting to even relatively minor stressors with intense affect. As such, they are especially suitable candidates for cognitive therapy. It should be emphasized here that, especially with borderline clients, the cognitive therapist must exercise caution against making the all too common error of "invalidating" the client's emotions. Described by Linehan (personal communication, November 13, 1986) as a possible etiological factor in the borderline's development, invalidation refers to the message that one's feelings are inappropriate, unacceptable, or even nonexistent. It is incumbent on the cognitive therapist to remain accepting of painful affect while challenging maladaptive beliefs. This can mean the difference between the client who is helped and the client who feels misunderstood and leaves therapy.

In their book on rational-emotive therapy, Walen et al. (1980) condense the irrational beliefs proposed by A. Ellis (1962) into the following derivative cognitions:

Things are awful.
I can't stand it.
I'm (or you're) a rotten person.

Clinical experience shows that most persons suffering from frequent and intense upset hold some or all of these beliefs, and a variety of studies supports this impression (e.g., Nelson, 1977; Smith, Houston,

& Zurawski, 1984). Cognitive restructuring involves using a variety of methods to show clients that (a) things may be unpleasant, but are seldom awful; (b) because a situation is undesirable does not mean that they cannot bear it; and (c) unnecessary upset and hostility can be avoided, and problems solved more effectively, if one evaluates behaviors rather than judging oneself or others.

The conviction that "things are awful" often stems from the prior belief that certain things, such as love or achievement, are needed (i.e., necessary for survival), when they are actually just strongly desired. Hence, we hear clients speaking of their "need" to be accepted by their peer group or saying that they "can't go on" without their loved one. Certainly, these ideas are strongly reinforced by popular songs, soap operas, and other cultural norms. It is no wonder that a person sincerely believing these ideas would take drastic measures to get these "needs" met. Cognitive therapy can be used effectively here to show the client that he or she can indeed survive with certain forms of frustration and that certainly no desire or want is in the life-or-death category to which the client had assigned it. This in large part requires helping clients to reduce their low frustration tolerance (Walen et al., 1980).

Remedying the demand for immediate gratification can be expected to significantly lower the danger of impulsive suicide attempts triggered by frustrated desires. It should be pointed out in this context that considering suicide in response to frustrated affiliative desires, though often taking an angry, demanding tone, may also be associated with fearful affect. Believing that they truly cannot survive without a strong, devoted other to care for them, these individuals may attempt suicide in a state of near panic. They are, in effect, saying, "I can never survive alone, and the fear is so great that I would rather die than experience it." As such, this individual represents a combination of the client who wishes to die to end the pain and the one who is making a desperate "cry for help."

Assertiveness. A common reason for "manipulative" behavior, whether in the form of suicidal behavior or otherwise, is inadequate ability to articulate desires and express feelings. In the absence of direct requests or emotional expression, what we find instead is "acting out." Assertiveness training can be one more effective means of providing alternatives to suicidal behavior as a goal-attaining behavior. Several guides are available for the conduct of assertiveness training, including Alberti and Emmons (1974) and Lange and Jakubowski (1976).

Case example. "Norma" was a 27-year-old divorced receptionist and mother of two who was referred by her family physician when no organic cause could be found for her headaches, insomnia, and frequent, involuntary vomiting. She also complained of chronic unhappiness and interpersonal difficulties both at work and in her social life. During her initial interview, she acknowledged only transient thoughts of passive suicide (e.g., "wishing I would get sick and die"). Current life stressors ranged from financial problems and pressures from being a single parent to vandalism in the neighborhood and car trouble. Her tendency was to speak at length of how "terrible" her problems were, to report feeling overwhelmed, and to say, "Why is it always me? I never get a break."

Therapy was initiated, and relaxation training, assertiveness training, cognitive restructuring, and problem-solving were effective in alleviating many of the autonomic and behavioral manifestations of Norma's anxiety disorder. Her first suicidal episode occurred several months into treatment. While dealing with her upset following the accidental death of her ex-husband, her grandmother died, she separated from her second husband, and she learned that her father had a possibly terminal illness. She began feeling overwhelmed and hopeless that she would ever have "the love I need." According to her report, she then obtained a pistol, loaded it with one shell, and on two occasions spun the chamber, placed the barrel to her temple, and pulled the trigger. She later recalled that when the gun did not fire she "figured it must not be my time" and put the weapon away.

At this point, therapy shifted from anxiety management and problem-solving to a combined focus on dependency issues and suicidal behavior as a coping strategy. Her motivations toward suicide were multiple and included: "I can't stand the thought of being alone;" "My children will be better off without me;" "I'm no good;" and "I'm just tired of all the shit." Each of these justifications was dealt with in turn, with the therapist pointing out the inherent fallacies and assisting with the development of rational alternatives. Unlike many other clients with personality disorders, Norma's suicidal thoughts and behaviors appeared private and did not seem to involve "manipulation" so much as low frustration tolerance and demands that her problems not exist.

However, the communication function emerged later—within the therapeutic relationship—when she had a second, similar, suicidal episode. In this instance, she had mailed a letter describing her "innermost feelings" to the therapist before again playing Russian roulette. Later exploration revealed that the motive (of which she was unaware) for both the letter and her parasuicide was to communicate to the therapist "just how bad I really feel." Norma said that, while she had felt accepted by the therapist, she felt too ashamed to express the full extent of her upset feelings during therapy sessions. This led to a discussion of her self-rejecting cognitions and catastrophic ideas about being abandoned if the therapist (or anyone else) should see "the real me."

These sessions proved successful in eliminating future suicidal episodes, permitting a shift in focus to her low frustration tolerance and upset-producing beliefs.

GENERAL PRINCIPLES IN THE TREATMENT OF SUICIDAL CLIENTS

In this chapter, we have examined suicide as a multifaceted, multidimensional phenomenon. It has been suggested that, because no common motivation has been identified underlying all suicidal behavior, the practitioner must be especially diligent in assessing the client for unique cognitive vulnerabilities and behavioral deficits that result in the threat of self-destruction and that can be targeted in therapy. We have seen evidence that suicidal depressed clients, more than other clients, show tendencies toward dichotomous thinking, rigidity, belief in the necessity of love and achievement, and other cognitive vulnerabilities. With the communication/control attempter or threatener, on the other hand, it appears important to deal explicitly with suicide as an interpersonal problem-solving strategy, with the treatment goal of helping the client to see fit to give up the suicide option by developing alternative, more advantageous, strategies.

This discussion would not be complete without some mention of the cognitions of the therapist. This topic is important because it relates to two vital aspects of therapy: treatment outcome and therapist well-being. As mentioned earlier, suicidal behavior often elicits negative reactions from therapists. Reasons for this may range from the stigma often attached to suicide to the fear of emotional trauma and possible litigation should the client commit suicide. This, combined with the lingering thought that the client may merely be "manipulating," adds up to a high likelihood of negative attitudes toward the client. Limbacher and Domino (1986) explore the complexities of attitudes toward suicide, pointing out that negative attitudes may interfere with the therapist's ability to help suicidal people (Ansel & McGee, 1971). This makes it imperative that the therapist thoroughly understand the dynamics of suicidal behavior and see that it can be irrational and "make sense" at the same time. Such understanding can be a helpful alternative to impatiently judging the client on the one hand or sympathizing with (and implicitly condoning) suicidal behavior on the other. An additional desirable attitude, helpful to therapist and client alike, is thoroughly understanding the principle of self-acceptance (Ellis, 1973). Firm insistence on evaluating behaviors but not human beings will help the therapist maintain appropriate compassion for the client and the client to learn an alternative to self-judgment and consequent self-destruction.

Finally, it would probably behoove most clinicians working with suicidal clients also to examine their beliefs about personal responsibility. Clinical wisdom among practitioners admonishes that it is not a matter of whether one of their clients will someday commit suicide, but of when. Therapists often live in constant fear of client suicide, a condition that, in keeping with the cognitive model of emotion, probably has rational and irrational components. While rationally wishing the best for our clients, we sometimes irrationally believe ourselves to have life-or-death power over them, such that if they commit suicide we would be to blame. Although it is the therapist's obligation to practice up to reasonable standards of competence, the clinician who feels responsible for the life of his or her client is at risk for taking that responsibility away from the client and for suffering excessive trauma should that client commit suicide. By thoroughly understanding the principle of personal responsibility for life and happiness, the therapist is in the best position to help the client experience him or herself as in control of his or her own fate and begin to change suicidal hopelessness into hope for the future.

Chapter 10
Treatment and Management of Suicidal Children and Adolescents

Chapter 6 provided information useful in evaluating suicide risk among young clients. Once risk has been identified, the therapist must respond in a maximally effective manner. Recognition of suicidal ideation and behaviors among children and adolescents may be particularly anxiety provoking for many mental health professionals. In fact, Pfeffer (1984) noted that clinicians may avoid dealing with suicide risk among children partly as a result of being unsure of appropriate interventions. This chapter is intended to decrease therapist anxiety (and, consequently, to increase the likelihood of effective intervention) by acquainting the reader with approaches for treating and managing children and adolescents who present with suicide risk. Furthermore, therapists engaged in treatment with suicidal youths are encouraged to consult additional resources (as is suggested in the reference section at the end of this book) for more extensive information on specific interventions.

It is also recommended that before reading this chapter the therapist become familiar with the response guidelines presented in Chapters 8 and 9. In those chapters, a distinction was made between crisis management and ongoing therapy with suicidal clients. Appropriate crisis management procedures include (a) increasing therapeutic activity, (b) delaying suicidal impulses, (c) instilling hope, (d) intervening in the client's environment, and (e) hospitalizing when indicated. In general, procedures described in Chapter 8 should also be followed with young clients. This chapter focuses on specific treatment issues for therapy with suicidal children and adolescents.

THERAPEUTIC ISSUES

Specific interventions should be chosen based on information gathered during the assessment phase. As seen in previous chapters, suicidal behavior is occasioned by an interaction of cognitive, behavioral, familial, and other influences. Identifying those variables that contribute to individual suicidal behavior facilitates the selection of target areas for intervention. Given the complex etiology of suicidal ideation and actions, effective treatment must necessarily be multifaceted. Thus, the therapist should be especially careful in completing a comprehensive evaluation that guides treatment selection.

The following sections describe therapeutic issues relevant specifically to the treatment of suicidal youth. Included are cognitive and behavioral areas for intervention, as well as environmental and supportive manipulations. In addition, suggestions for facilitating and maintaining treatment gains are made.

Concepts of Death

Pfeffer (1986) described the important role of children's conceptualization of death and related constructs in the assessment of suicide risk. Children's ideas about death are formulated by an interaction of cognitive abilities, maturation, and experience. Very young children (less than 5 years old) typically consider death a reversible and temporary state. Later (approximately between the ages of 5 and 9), children recognize the permanence of death, but do not yet associate death with themselves. After about age 12, increased abstract reasoning facilitates an understanding of death as an inevitable part of life (Nagy, 1948, as cited in Papalia & Olds, 1986).

Empirical evidence indicates that children typically are able to discuss their ideas and experiences related to death. However, it appears that intense preoccupation with death differentiates suicidal from nonsuicidal children (Pfeffer, 1986). Pfeffer (1986) recommends that such preoccupations be regarded as suicide risk indicators, but also notes that such thoughts may be typical of children who have suffered recent losses. In all cases, excessive and chronic thoughts of death and related concepts should be addressed by the therapist.

When young children consider death as a temporary and reversible state, they may be likely to view suicide as a solution to intolerable stress. Not understanding the potential finality of self-destructive behavior, suicidal acts may be seen as a viable alternative to a present state of discomfort. Preoccupation with death may also arise as a result of experiencing deaths of significant others, or as a result of anxieties stemming from losses such as parental separation and divorce.

Education regarding death and related concepts may be one treatment component in such cases. Information should be communicated to children using age-appropriate language, with special attention to making sure concepts are explained in contexts relevant to the individual child. Depending on the child, the following issues may be appropriate: (a) death as a naturally-occurring event, (b) death as final and irreversible, (c) the availability of alternative solutions to distress, and (d) the impact of death on significant others. Of course, interventions should include efforts to decrease external sources of stress to the child (as discussed in a later section).

Recall the case of 7-year-old Mark, as presented in Chapter 6. The initial interview indicated that Mark viewed death as a means of avoiding the hospital for medical treatment. In addition, Mark felt that he would ease his mother's burdens by not creating additional financial expenses if he were not to receive his treatment. Subsequent interviews revealed that Mark saw his own death as a way to make things easier for his mother. Treatment then focused on several issues, including the impact Mark's death would have on his mother. Mark was taught to identify and evaluate various options regarding the decision about his medical treatment. In addition, time was spent teaching Mark about the finality of death. This concept was introduced to Mark by discussing the death of his pet dog, which he had experienced some 2 years earlier.

Adolescent Immortality and Romanticizing Death

Many adolescents regard themselves as immune to harm (e.g., the "personal fable" as discussed in Chapter 6), and frequently engage in reckless and dangerous behaviors. These types of clients may benefit from education regarding the mortality of others in their age group, as evidenced by statistics of teen deaths by automobile accidents. Such behaviors should be considered serious indicators of distress and efforts should be made by the therapist to evaluate the function of such extreme behaviors. For some adolescents, peer attention may serve to maintain dangerous behaviors. In those cases, education regarding consequences may be useful. However, other youths may behave recklessly as a means of communicating distress. Intervention in such cases should include training the client more adaptive ways to deal with problems, and may include areas such as communication, problem-solving, and relaxation skills.

Adolescents may also view suicidal behavior as a desirable or "ulti-mate" way to communicate their feelings to significant others. Thera-pists should assess a suicidal adolescent's views about the impact his or her death would have on others, probing for 'messages' the youth may want to send to specific persons. Treatment may then focus on training more adaptive ways to communicate emotions to significant others.

Functional Analysis

In many cases, self-destructive behavior among children and adoles-cents may be examined in terms of the variables that serve to elicit and maintain them. As discussed in Chapter 6, a complete analysis of the behavior, including the antecedents and consequences, may yield a powerful therapeutic intervention. While many behavioral interven-tions have focused on the reduction and elimination of self-injurious behavior (e.g., Keefe & Ward, 1981), it is the behavioral approach of functional analysis that may be applied to a suicidal youth's behaviors that is of present interest. Characteristics of this approach include (a) identifying target behaviors that are measured in quantifiable terms, (b) repeating measurement over time, (c) designing treatment to meet individual needs, (d) systematically evaluating treatment on an ongo-ing basis, and (e) programming generalization and maintenance of treatment gains (Keefe & Ward, 1981).

As noted, the hallmark of behavioral treatment is the design of ther-apeutic intervention based on the individual needs of the client. A complete functional analysis serves to identify not only the specific en-vironmental variables controlling suicidal behavior, but also suggests areas for intervention. Examples of various treatment components are presented below.

Cognitive Therapy

The role of affective states in suicidal behavior has been clearly dem-onstrated and has been discussed throughout this book. For youths suffering from feelings of depression and hopelessness, appropriate cognitive therapies may be used.

The use of cognitive therapies requires that the therapist be aware of the child's level of cognitive functioning, the specific cognitions re-lated to suicidal behaviors and ideation, and how to alter those cogni-tions. Analyses concerning how particular cognitions serve to elicit and maintain problem behaviors facilitate their modification.

The treatment of depression may take many forms, including medication and cognitive therapy. The limits of this chapter do not allow a comprehensive discussion of treating depression. The reader is encouraged to consult clinical resources specific to the treatment of childhood and adolescent depression. Feelings of hopelessness may also be addressed by engaging in cognitive restructuring with the youth. Negative expectancies may be identified, addressed, challenged, and modified. Environments may be manipulated in order to enhance the likelihood that pleasurable activities will occur at an increasing rate and that clients will attain some positive interactions with their environment. For example, Foster and DeLawyer (1987) have been involved with identifying social skills necessary for young children to be interpersonally effective with their peers. Such research findings may be instrumental in teaching critical behaviors to children so that they may increase their positive experiences with those in their environment.

Another critical area involved in the treatment of suicidal youths involves self-concept. The way a child or adolescent perceives him or herself and his or her effect on the environment may contribute to feelings of depression and hopelessness. Treatment, then, may focus on increasing the child's self-esteem by using strategies such as increasing the frequency of positive self-statements, increasing feelings of self-control, and training social and problem-solving skills. For example, Pope, McHale and Craighead (1988) have proposed a package of interventions designed to increase child and adolescent self-esteem. Their approach is characterized by training the child to examine the self, to frame self-concept within a positive valence, and to increase skills necessary for effectiveness in the environment.

Behavioral

Assessment often may indicate that a distressed youth lacks the behaviors necessary to be maximally effective in his or her environment. Such ineffectiveness contributes to feelings of diminished self-esteem, depression, and hopelessness. Children may demonstrate deficits in any number of important arenas, including social and academic settings. As a result, the therapist may include skills training in a specific domain as part of treatment.

Children who appear to be socially unskilled may benefit from training in interaction skills. Increasing the likelihood that peer interactions will occur may decrease feelings of isolation and loneliness. Training problem-solving skills may also increase the youth's feelings of control over his or her environment. As a result, self-esteem may be enhanced. Problem-solving skills may also aid the youth in alleviating stressors in an effective way. Youths who have little control over their hostility and emotional outbursts may benefit from anger control training (e.g., Feindler & Ecton, 1986). Skills training in anger control involves teaching youths to identify their individual responses to provocative situations, and then training subsequent behaviors to defuse their anger responses. The approach includes various cognitive strategies that are presented in ways suitable for adolescents and modifiable for younger children.

Family

Perhaps one of the most important treatment issues for suicidal children and adolescents involves the youth's family. A comprehensive assessment serves to indicate how family members contribute to the etiology and maintenance of suicidal behavior. Involving family members in the treatment of suicidal youths requires an understanding of the existing family system. A determination of the family's ability to contribute to treatment in a facilitative manner must be made by the therapist.

In families where parental support is available for the suicidal child, a critical role in treatment may be fulfilled. Parents may be used to increase protection of the child from self-harm. This may be achieved by instructing the parent in ways to recognize danger signs of problematic behaviors. Parents may be trained in appropriate and effective ways to intervene, along with training to discriminate when they should contact professionals. In addition, parents may be instrumental in alleviating potential hazards by removing physical items such as firearms, medications, and poisons from accessible places.

However, therapists treating suicidal children from seriously dysfunctional families may find the family unit the focus of intervention (Fishman & Rosman, 1981). While the youth may be the identified patient, the family may be severely distressed and unable to provide the emotional support needed for the suicidal youth. In such cases, the therapist must identify the role of the family in maintaining maladaptive behaviors, and intervene at the necessary levels. Stressful home environments may be characterized by problems ranging from parental depression, psychosis, or other pathologies, to marital conflict and violence.

Supportive Interventions

Additional interventions that may be used involve significant others in the youth's environment. For example, group therapy may be particularly effective with suicidal adolescents (Curran, 1987; Davis, 1983;

Ross & Motto, 1984). Gaining support and understanding from one's peers may be especially valuable for adolescents, who often mistrust and/or resent adult guidance. In addition, acceptance from one's peer group may be invaluable in reducing the stigma felt by engaging in suicidal behaviors.

Often, children and adolescents relate to one person in their environment particularly well. It would behoove the therapist to involve that person in therapy, offering instruction in ways to increase and maintain adaptive behaviors on the part of the client. For example, a child's favorite art teacher may be asked to participate in treatment by involving the child in pleasurable activities. Activities could be structured in ways that success would be attainable, thus increasing the child's contact with environmental rewards.

Efforts should be made to identify sources of stress for the child, and interventions devised to decrease stress, especially in times of crisis. For example, severely depressed youths experiencing failures in school as a result of demanding coursework are likely to benefit from therapist involvement in restructuring school activities. It should be noted that such rearrangements should be temporary, with ultimate goals of increasing the youth's ability to function within the existing demands of their environment.

School Intervention

Mental health professionals have become increasingly involved in providing therapeutic services in the school environment. One such area of involvement concerns suicide. With an increased public awareness of the threat of adolescent suicide, many schools have taken a proactive stance by instituting educational programs in an effort to prevent suicides from occurring. In fact, Slenkovich (1986) reported that a school district in Oregon was held legally responsible in the suicidal death of a 14-year-old student while on school premises. The court had ruled that the school had a "duty to provide suicide prevention training to employees, and that it failed to do so." School involvement has ranged from preventive programs to interventions, and postventions (Ross, 1980; Thompson, 1988).

Poland (1989) has outlined an extensive model for the implementation of programs designed for the prevention, intervention, and postvention of suicide within the school system. The model is extremely comprehensive and includes specific techniques and issues for implementing the program. The reader is encouraged to consult this definitive text on school intervention. Joan (1986) also provides a complete curriculum for mental health professionals that provides specific techniques for increasing awareness of suicidal signs among adolescents and for intervention.

Generalization and Maintenance

As with all therapeutic interventions, efforts should be made to facilitate the generalization and maintenance of treatment gains. The role of the family in maintaining treatment gains cannot be overemphasized. Family members can encourage adaptive behaviors, model teach new behaviors, and reinforce appropriate behaviors. Therapists should include family instruction as part of any treatment plan with suicidal youths. In addition, youths should be equipped with skills necessary for effective functioning so that naturally occurring reinforcers may be experienced.

HOSPITALIZATION

Hospitalization may be necessary in cases where outpatient therapy is not the treatment of choice. In fact, many authors recommend that children and adolescents who engage in suicidal behaviors be hospitalized, and that therapists should prefer to err on the side of being overly cautious when in doubt (see Davis, 1983).

The ultimate criterion for such a decision concerns the safety of the suicidal youth. If the youth's family is dysfunctional and nonsupportive, the client may be better protected in residential placement. Also, youths experiencing severe distress or psychosis should be considered at high risk and steps should be taken to assure protection from self-harm. Some youths may benefit from medical interventions with antipsychotic or antidepressant medications.

It is strongly recommended that therapists maintain contact with their clients once hospitalization has occurred. Such continuity is essential to the youth's perception of therapist concern, and may be instrumental in treatment. Therapists may be involved in treatment planning for hospitalized children as members of a multidisciplinary team including physicians, social workers, nurses, and other therapists.

SUMMARY

In sum, there are several critical issues in the treatment of suicidal children and adolescents. First and foremost, all suicidal behaviors, including verbal gestures and physical acts, should be considered seriously. Such behaviors are indications of distress among children, even when they appear to function as manipulations of other individuals.

Second, treatment plans should be based on comprehensive evaluations. Given the complex interaction of variables contributing to suicidal behavior, effective treatment can occur only when multiple determinants are considered and addressed. Each case should be considered in regard to the specific needs presented by the individual.

Treating suicidal youth requires that therapists involve family members and significant others in assessment and therapy. Such individuals play a critical role not only in assessing the etiology of an individual child's suicidal behaviors, but also in the effective implementation of intervention strategies.

Many investigators, including Pfeffer (1986) and Richman (1981), have emphasized that the treatment of suicidal children be conducted by experienced and highly qualified professionals. It is our hope that the information provided in this chapter serves the purpose of introducing the mental health professional to the special issues involved in treating suicidal youth. The treatment issues discussed here are only briefly described, and therapists interested in providing services to suicidal youths should procure specific and extensive training. Finally, it is our hope that the present discussion will allow the therapist to (a) recognize suicidal behaviors among young clients, (b) plan effective treatment strategies, and (c) refer youths to other professionals as needed.

Chapter 11
Survivors and Final Considerations

This book presents the current research and clinical literature to help mental health professionals better assess and treat suicidal clients. One major theme is that a careful and thorough evaluation is necessary to evaluate the potential risk for suicide. This evaluation begins with considerations of the individual's demographic characteristics such as age, sex, and marital status, and proceeds through consideration of his or her personal and family history, and current psychological features. Among the many factors discussed, a history of prior suicide attempts combined with current feelings of hopelessness suggests a high level of risk. Throughout the evaluation, it is essential that the clinical information and decision process be well documented. Case law does not require a therapist to be omniscient and unerring. The emerging body of case law does require, however, that the professional exercise a reasonable degree of professional judgment and care in the assessment and treatment of a potentially suicidal client. This judgment must be documented in order for the court to accept a therapist's decision (*Johnson v. United States*, 1981).

SURVIVORS OF SUICIDE

Working with a potentially suicidal client requires a continuing evaluation of the person's risk and consideration of the various treatment options. Unfortunately, regardless of how clinically sensitive, responsible, and skilled a therapist may be, a client may commit suicide. Suicide can occur despite everyone's best efforts to prevent it. If a suicide occurs, the mental health professional should be sensitive to the potential impact on him or herself, colleagues, organization, and the family

and friends of the victim. The impact of a suicidal death can be trau-
matic. Andress and Corey (1978) found that approximately 25% of suicides occur either while the victim was speaking to someone else by
telephone or in the presence of another person. This relatively high
level of social involvement reflects that suicides may be a form of interpersonal communication and have significant interpersonal impact. These
witnesses receive a lifelong memory of the person's death. If a suicide
has happened within an interpersonal context, the witness should receive intensive crisis-oriented counseling to help him or her deal with
the trauma of the death and the potential feelings of responsibility for
not having prevented it.

If a suicide occurs in an inpatient setting, hospital procedures often
require a staff review or psychological autopsy of the victim. This formal procedure helps identify any errors of omission or commission by
the staff that may have occurred before the person's death. The review
can improve care for other high-risk patients by identifying alternative
procedures for suicidal patients. Equally important, it can serve as a
therapeutic session to help the staff discuss their feelings of loss, anger, and responsibility over the suicide. Research has shown that therapists who have lost a patient through suicide often suffer significant
symptoms of stress (Chemtob, Hamada, Bauer, Torigoe, & Kinney, 1988).
The support of other concerned professionals and a realistic discussion
of the limits of their ability to prevent suicide can be a very important
therapeutic tool to help the professional staff deal with the impact of
the suicide.

The theme of personal responsibility for the death of another individual needs to be explored in a sensitive and supportive manner.
Sharing of these feelings among the staff can help lessen the feeling
that any one individual has failed and that he or she could not be
helpful to other patients. Working with psychiatrically disturbed individuals is stressful enough without having to cope with the death of a
patient. Therefore, it is very important that the professional staff process and deal with their mixed feelings if a death occurs among one of
their patients. Failure to therapeutically address these issues can lead
to further stress and eventual burn-out. Perhaps the most therapeutic
intervention available is the retrospective discussion of the patient's
suicide risk and steps taken to reduce this risk. An honest evaluation
of the limits of a professional staff's responsibility to prevent suicide if
all appropriate steps have been taken can be very important to help
the staff cope with the death.

The family and immediate friends of the person who commits suicide suffer even greater trauma. The person who has committed suicide has chosen death as the final means to cope with his or her life

problems. Unfortunately, this choice often leaves a lifetime legacy of guilt and anger among the people who survive. While the death of a family member always causes pain, a death by suicide may induce even more intense feelings of loss, guilt, and anger. The family members often ruminate about their acts and their relations with the suicidal person, looking for clues and choices that could have led to saving the life. The survivors must deal with both the death and loss of that person from their life as well as the manner in which the person died. Feelings of shame and social stigma occur. Grief over a nonsuicidal death, such as from a car accident or illness, can last for as long as 2 years before a person generally resumes his or her prior level of psychological functioning. Grieving over a suicide may last longer unless peer support groups or professionals intervene.

Because of the major impact of suicide on surviving family members, support groups have been formed for survivors to assist in coping with their loss. The American Association of Suicidology (AAS) has listings of over 120 suppost groups for survivors of suicide. These groups, based on a recent survey, share the goals of education, helping survivors ventilate their feelings, providing social support, and referring survivors for professional help when warranted. They are usually led by a supervising therapist and facilitators who are themselves survivors (Fisher, 1988). Newsletters entitled *Afterwards* and *Survivors of Suicide Newsletter* provide valuable information for these groups and for professionals who work with suicide.

Shneidman (1967) has identified three stages of intervention with suicidal persons: prevention of suicide, intervention during crisis, and postvention. The preceding chapters have provided some suggestions for prevention and intervention. Postvention consists of activities to reduce the trauma in the lives of survivors of suicide. The goal of postvention is to help survivors live more productive and less distressful lives than they might otherwise. F. V. Wenz suggests 11 principles for postvention work:

1. Be trusting.
2. Be available to the survivor.
3. Offer your physical presence even if in silence.
4. Discourage the survivor's guilt feelings such as, "If I had just done this."
5. Show your sympathy, understanding, and warmth.
6. Discourage self-pity by the survivor.
7. Encourage the survivor to express his or her real feelings, fears, anxieties, and loneliness.
8. Encourage activities.

9. Help guide the survivor in formulating his or her immediate future.
10. Offer spiritual support.
11. Encourage the survivor to take time to accept the trauma and shock of the suicide.

Integrating the survivor into a support group and monitoring the survivor's medical and psychological condition are two important additional strategies.

The anniversaries of the death of a loved one are particularly difficult times because of the powerful and mixed feelings the survivors may experience. Survivors may even contemplate committing suicide to join a dead family member. The mental health professional should be aware of these dates and help clients and families anticipate and accept the heightened level of sadness and grief they may experience on these anniversaries. With them, as with professional colleagues, the issue of personal responsibility for another person's life needs to be thoroughly explored.

The previous chapters should help prepare the mental health professional to better assess and lessen the risk that a client will successfully commit suicide. Remember, most people who contemplate suicide do not act. Most people who attempt suicide survive. Over 80% percent of people who attempt suicide never die by suicide. If we can be sensitive to the early warning signs of suicide risk and aid our clients to successfully cope with their immediate crises, most will live to have a full and long life.

Appendix
Drug and Chemical Ingestion Lethality

Drug[a]	LD$_{50}$[b]	How Supplied	Lethal Range for a 120 lb. Person in caps, tabs or ounces	Lethal Range for a 170 lb. Person in caps, tabs or ounces
Acetaminophen				
(Tylenol-Reg. Strength)	200–1000 mg/Kg	325 mg tab	34–168	47–237
*(Tylenol-Extra Strength)	200–1000 mg/Kg	500 mg tab	22–109	31–155
*(Anacin-3)	200–1000 mg/Kg	500 mg tab	22–109	31–155
	140 mg/Kg causes liver damage		23 reg. strength 16 extra strength	33 reg. strength 22 extra strength
Allerest				
Composed of:				
2 mg Chlorphenirainine	25–250 mg/Kg	tab	78	110
18.7 mg Phenylpropanolamine	2000 mg			
4 mg Chlorpheniramine	25–250 mg/Kg	cap	29	41
*50 mg Phenylpropanolamine	2000 mg			
Alprazolam	approx. 8000 mg	0.5 mg tab	12,457	17,669
(Xanax)		1 mg tab	6,229	8,834
Amitriptyline HCl	35–50 mg/Kg	10 mg tab	191–273	271–387
(Elavil)		25 mg tab	76–109	108–155
		50 mg tab	38–55	54–77
		75 mg tab	25–36	36–52
		100 mg tab	19–27	27–39
		150 mg tab	13–18	18–26
*Amphetamine	100–200 mg	5 mg tab	20–40	20–40
(Dextroamphetamine)	(not prorated by	10 mg cap	10–20	10–20
(Dexedrine)	body weight)	15 mg cap	7–13	7–13
*Amytal	1500 mg	50 mg tab	23	33
	(not prorated by body weight)	100 mg tab	12	17
*Amytal Sodium	1500 mg	65 mg tab	18	25
	(not prorated by body weight)	200 mg cap	6	8
Arsenate of Lead	100–500 mg	—	78–389 mg	110–552 mg

143

Drug[a]	LD$_{50}$[b]	How Supplied	Lethal Range for a 120 lb. Person in caps, tabs or ounces	Lethal Range for a 170 lb. Person in caps, tabs or ounces
Arsenic	200 mg (not prorated by body weight)	—	156 mg	221 mg
Artane (Trihexyphenidyl)	100–1000 mg (not prorated by body weight)	2 mg tab 5 mg cap	39–390 16–160	55–550 22–220
Asendin (Amoxapine)	50–500 mg/Kg	50 mg tab 100 mg tab 150 mg tab	55–550 27–270 18–180	77–770 39–390 25–250
*Depakene (Valproic Acid)	50–500 mg/Kg	250 mg cap	11–110	15–150
Desipramine HCl (Norpramin) (Pertorfrane)	35–50 mg/Kg	25 mg tab 50 mg tab 75 mg tab 100 mg tab 150 mg tab	76–109 38–55 25–36 19–27 12–18	108–155 54–77 36–52 27–39 18–25
*Dexol Bleach	5 ml to 30 ml 1/6 to 1 oz	liquid	1/6 to 1 oz	¼ to 1¼ oz
Diazepam HCl (Valium)	50–500 mg/Kg	2 mg tab 5 mg tab 10 mg tab	1,360–13,630 545–5,450 273–2,730	1,933–19,330 773–7,730 387–3,870
Dilantin (Phenytoin)	100–500 mg/Kg	100 mg cap	55–273	77–770
Diphenhydramine HCl (Benadryl)	20–40 mg/Kg	25 mg cap 50 mg cap	44–88 22–44	62–124 31–62
*Doriden (Glutethamide)	100–500 mg/Kg	250 mg tab 500 mg tab	22–109 11–55	31–155 16–77
Doxepin HCl (Sinequan, Adepin)	35–50 mg/Kg	10 mg cap 25 mg cap 50 mg cap 75 mg cap 100 mg cap 150 mg cap	191–273 76–109 38–55 25–36 19–28 13–18	271–387 108–155 54–77 36–52 27–39 18–26
*Dramamine (Dimenhydrinate)	25–250 mg/Kg	50 mg tab	27–270	39–390
Drawing Ink	480–960 cc 16–32 oz	liquid	12–24	18–36
Dristan tablets Composed of: 2 mg Chlorpheniramine 5 mg Phenylephrine 325 mg Aspirin 16.2 mg Caffeine	25–250 mg/Kg 1000 mg 200–500 mg/Kg 183–250 mg/Kg	tab	65	92
*Dristan capsules Composed of: 4 mg Chlorpheniramine 50 mg Phenylephrine	25–250 mg/Kg 1000 mg	cap	16	22
Elavil see Amitriptyline	—	—		

Drug[a]	LD$_{50}$[b]	How Supplied	Lethal Range for a 120 lb. Person in caps, tabs or ounces	Lethal Range for a 170 lb. Person in caps, tabs or ounces
Empirin see Aspirin	—	—		
*Empirin #1, #2, #3, #4 Composed of: 325 mg Aspirin Codeine (8, 15, 30, 60mg)	200–500 mg/Kg 500–800 mg	#1 tab #2 tab #3 tab #4 tab	51–82 26–41 13–21 7–11	73–117 36–58 18–29 9–15
*Equagesic Composed of: 250 mg Aspirin 25 mg Ethoheptazine 150 mg Meprobamate	200–500 mg/Kg 1000 mg 100–500 mg/Kg	tab	19–23	28–33
*Equanil (Meprobamate)	100–500 mg/Kg	200 mg tab 400 mg tab	27–136 14–68	39–193 20–97
*Ethchlorvynol (Placidyl)	100–500 mg/Kg	200 mg cap 500 mg cap 750 mg cap	27–136 11–55 7–35	39–193 16–78 10–50
*Ethinamate (Valmid)	100–500 mg/Kg	500 mg cap	11–55	16–78
Etrafon, Triavil (Amitriptyline) (Trilafon)	35–50 mg/Kg 15–150 mg/Kg	2–10 tab 2–25 tab 4–10 tab 4–25 tab 4–50 tab	191–226 76–100 191–195 76–93 38–51	271–320 108–142 271–276 108–133 54–72
*Excedrin Composed of: 250 mg Aspirin 250 mg Acetaminophen 65 mg Caffeine	200–500 mg/Kg 200–1000 mg/Kg 183–250 mg/Kg	tab	19–48	28–68
*Fiorinal Composed of: 50 mg Butalbital 200 mg Aspirin 40 mg Caffeine	200–500 mg/Kg 200–500 mg/Kg 183–250 mg/Kg	tab cap	23–31	33–44
Flurazepam HCl see Dalmane	—	—		
Furniture Polish (80% Kerosene)	30–480 cc 1–16 oz	liquid	1–12 oz	1–18 oz
*Glutethamide see Doriden	—	—		
Haldol (Haloperidol)	15–150 mg/Kg	0.5 mg tab 1 mg tab 2 mg tab 5 mg tab 10 mg tab 20 mg tab	1,635–16,350 818–8,180 409–4,090 164–1,640 82–820 41–410	2,319–23,190 1,160–11,600 580–5,800 232–2,320 116–1,160 58–580
Hydroxyzine HCl see Atarax	—	—		
Imipramine HCl (Tofranil)	35–50 mg/Kg	10 mg tab 25 mg tab 50 mg tab	191–273 76–109 38–55	271–387 108–155 54–78

Drug[a]	LD$_{50}$[b]	How Supplied	Lethal Range for a 120 lb. Person in caps, tabs or ounces	Lethal Range for a 170 lb. Person in caps, tabs or ounces
Iodine, Tincture	2000 ml 3.5 oz	liquid	3 oz	4 oz
Librium see Chlordiazepoxide HCl	—	—		
Lighter Fluid Composed of: petroleum distallates	30–250 cc 1–8 oz	liquid	1–6 oz	1–9 oz
Lithium Carbonate	serum level of 3–4 mEg/L	300 mg cap 300 mg tab	Serum level can be reached with as few as 15–20 caps	Serum level can be reached with as few as 15–20 caps
Lomotil Composed of: 2.5 mg Diphenoxylate HCl 0.025 mg Atropine Sulfate	200 mg	tab	62	88
Lorazepam see Ativan	—	—		
Loxapine (Loxitane)	50–500 mg/Kg	5 mg cap 10 mg cap 25 mg cap 50 mg cap	550–5,500 275–2,750 110–1,100 55–550	770–7,700 385–3,850 154–1,540 77–770
Ludiomil (Maprotiline HCl)	35–50 mg/Kg	25 mg tab 50 mg tab	76–109 38–55	108–155 54–78
Mellaril (Thioridazine HCl)	15–150 mg/Kg	10 mg tab 25 mg tab 50 mg tab 100 mg tab 150 mg tab 200 mg tab	82–820 33–330 16–160 8–80 6–60 4–40	116–1,160 46–460 23–230 12–120 9–90 6–60
*Meperidine HCl see Demerol	—	—		
*Meprobamate (Miltown, Equanil, Meprospan)	100–500 mg/Kg	200 mg tab 400 mg tab	27–136 14–68	39–193 20–97
Mercury salts (liquid Mercury is *not* toxic to the body since it is not absorbed)	500–1000 mg (not prorated by body weight)	found in insecticides	500–1,000 mg	500–1,000 mg
*Methadone (Dolophine HCl)	100 mg (not prorated by body weight)	5 mg tab 10 mg tab	16 8	22 11
Methanol	60–250 ml	liquid	2–6 oz	2–9 oz
Methapryilene HCl	50 mg/Kg	25 mg tab	109	155
Methaqualone (Quaalude)	100–500 mg/Kg	150 mg tab 300 mg tab	37–183 19–93	52–260 26–130
*Methylphenidate HCl (Ritalin)	200 mg	5 mg tab 10 mg tab 20 mg tab	31 16 8	44 22 11

Drug[a]	LD$_{50}$[b]	How Supplied	Lethal Range for a 120 lb. Person in caps, tabs or ounces	Lethal Range for a 170 lb. Person in caps, tabs or ounces
Methyprylon (Noludar)	100–500 mg/Kg	50 mg tab 200 mg tab 300 mg cap	109–545 27–136 18–91	155–773 39–194 26–129
Miltown see Meprobamate	—	—		
Mistletoe Composed of: Tryamine Betaphenethylamine	"considered dangerous"	berries	unknown	unknown
Moban (Molindone HCl)	15–150 mg/Kg	5 mg tab 10 mg tab 25 mg tab 50 mg tab 100 mg tab	164–1,640 82–820 33–330 16–160 8–80	232–2,320 116–1,160 46–460 23–230 12–120
Mysoline (Primidone)	100–500 mg/Kg	50 mg tab 250 mg tab	109–545 22–109	155–773 31–155
*Nail Polish (Toluene)	5–30 cc 1/6–1 oz	liquid	1/6 to 1 oz	1/4 to 1 1/4 oz
Nail Polish Remover (Acetone)	30–240 cc 1–8 oz	liquid	1–6 oz	1–8 oz
Nardil (Phenelzine SO$_4$)	25–100 mg/Kg	15 mg tab	91–364	129–517
Navane (Thiothixene HCl)	15–150 mg/Kg	1 mg cap 2 mg cap 5 mg cap 10 mg cap 20 mg cap	820–8,200 410–4,100 164–1,640 82–820 41–410	1,160–11,600 580–5,800 232–2,320 116–1,160 58–580
*Nembutal (Pentobarbital)	1000 mg (not prorated by body weight)	50 mg cap 100 mg cap	16 8	22 11
*Noctec see Chloral Hydrate	—	—		
Nodoz Composed of: 100 mg Caffeine	183–250 mg/Kg	tab	100–136	141–193
Noludar see Methyprylon	—	—		
Norpramin see Desipramine HCl	—	—		
Nortriptyline HCl (Aventyl, Pamelor)	35–50 mg/Kg	10 mg cap 25 mg cap 75 mg cap	191–273 76–109 25–36	271–387 108–155 36–52
Nytol (Pryilamine maleate)	40 mg/Kg	25 mg tab	87	124
Oleander leaves	3000 mg (not prorated by body weight)	—	2,336 mg	3,313 mg

Drug[a]	LD$_{50}$[b]	How Supplied	Lethal Range for a 120 lb. Person in caps, tabs or ounces	Lethal Range for a 170 lb. Person in caps, tabs or ounces
Oxazepam (Serax)	50–500 mg/Kg	10 mg cap 15 mg cap 30 mg cap	273–2,730 182–1,820 91–910	387–3,870 258–2,580 129–1,290
Paint thinner	"several ounces"	liquid	several ounces	several ounces
Pamelor see Nortriptyline HCl	—	—		
*Paraldehyde	30–100 cc 1–3 oz	liquid	1–2 oz	1–3.3 oz
Parnate (Tranycypromine SO$_4$)	25–100 mg/Kg	10 mg tab	136–545	193–773
Pemoline see Cylert	—	—		
*Pentazocine (Talwin)	300 mg (not prorated by body weight)	50 mg tab	5	7
*Pentobarbital (Nembutal)	1000 mg (not prorated by body weight)	50 mg cap 100 mg cap	16 8	22 11
Percodan (Oxycodone)	500 mg (not prorated by body weight)	4.5 mg tab 2.25 mg tab	78 156	110 220
Perfume Alcohol, methyl	60–250 cc 2–8 oz	liquid	2–6 oz	2–9 oz
Perphenazine HCl (Trilafon)	15–150 mg/Kg	2 mg tab 4 mg tab 8 mg tab 16 mg tab	409–4,090 205–2,050 102–1,020 51–510	580–5,800 290–2,900 145–1,450 73–730
Phenelzine SO$_4$ see Nardil	—	—		
Phenobarbital	1500 mg	15 mg tab 30 mg tab 60 mg tab 100 mg tab	78 39 20 12	110 55 28 17
Phenytoin see Dilantin	—	—		
Placidyl see Ethchlorvynol	—	—		
Potassium Cyanate	840 mg/Kg	powder		
Prazepam (Centrax)	50–500 mg/Kg	5 mg tab 10 mg tab	273–2,730 137–1,370	387–3,870 194–1,940
Propa-pH (Benzoyl Peroxide)	250 mg/Kg	cream 30 gm tubes	6.5 tubes	9 tubes
*Propoxyphene napsylate see Darvocet-N	—	—		
*Propoxyphene HCl see Darvon	—	—		

Drug[a]	LD$_{50}$[b]	How Supplied	Lethal Range for a 120 lb. Person in caps, tabs or ounces	Lethal Range for a 170 lb. Person in caps, tabs or ounces
Protriptyline HCl (Vivacti)	35–50 mg/Kg	5 mg tab 10 mg tab	382–546 191–273	542–774 271–387
Pyrilamine maleate	40 mg/Kg	25 mg tab	87	124
Quaalude see Methaqualone	—	—		
Quiet World Composed of: 227 mg Aspirin 162 mg Acetaminophen 25 mg Pyrilamine maleate	200–500 mg/Kg 200–1000 mg/Kg 40 mg/Kg	tab	48–58	68–83
Rat Poison (Warfarin)	10–100 mg daily	(single dose not dangerous; it takes *repeated* ingestions)		
Ritalin see Methylphenidate	—	—		
*Robaxin (Methocarbamol)	50–500 mg/Kg	500 mg tab 750 mg tab	5–50 4–40	8–80 6–60
Seconal (Secobarbital)	2000 mg (not prorated by body weight)	50 mg cap 100 mg cap	31 16	44 22
Serax see Oxazepam	—	—		
Shaving Lotion Composed of: Alcohol, methyl	600–800 cc 20–27 oz	liquid	20–27 oz	20–27 oz
Silicone Shoe Waterproofer	30–480 cc 1–16 oz	liquid	1–12 oz	1–18 oz
Sinequan see Doxepin HCl	—	—		
Sleepeze (Pyrilamine maleate)	40 mg/Kg	25 mg tab	87	124
Sodium Hydroxide	5000 mg (not prorated by body weight)	—		
Sominex (Pyrilamine maleate)	40 mg/Kg	25 mg tab	87	124
Sominex-2 (Diphenhydramine HCl)	20–40 mg/Kg	25 mg tab	44–88	62–124
Stelazine see Trifluoperazine	—	—		
*Sudafed (Pseudoephedrine)	1000 mg (not prorated by body weight)	30 mg tab 60 mg tab 120 mg tab	26 13 7	36 18 9
*Talwin see Pentazocine	—	—		
Tegretol see Carbamezine	—	—		

Drug[a]	LD$_{50}$[b]	How Supplied	Lethal Range for a 120 lb. Person in caps, tabs or ounces	Lethal Range for a 170 lb. Person in caps, tabs or ounces
Ten-O-Six Lotion	32 oz	liquid	24 oz	36 oz
Thioridazine HCl see Mellaril	—	—		
Thiothixene HCl see Navane	—	—		
Thorazine see Chlorpromazine HCl	—	—		
Tofranil see Imipramine HCl	—	—		
Tranyl cypromine SO$_4$ (Parnate)	25–100 mg/Kg	10 mg tab	136–545	193–773
*Tricos	2000–10,000 mg (not prorated by body weight)	750 mg tab	2–12	3–17
Trifluoperazine (Stelazine)	15–150 mg/Kg	1 mg tab 2 mg tab 5 mg tab 10 mg tab	818–8,180 409–4,090 164–1,640 82–820	1,160–11,600 580–5,800 232–2,320 116–1,160
Trilafon see Perphenazine	—	—		
*Tuinal Composed of: 50 mg Amobarbital 50 mg Secobarbital	1500 mg 1500 mg (not prorated by body weight)	100 mg cap	12	17
Tylenol, Tylenol *Extra Strength see Acetaminophen	—	—		
Valium see Diazepam HCl	—	—		
*Valmid see Ethinamate	—	—		
*Valproic Acid (Depakene)	50–500 mg/Kg	250 mg cap	11–100	15–150
Vivarin Composed of: 200 mg Caffeine	183–250 mg/Kg	tab	50–69	71–97
Vivactil see Protriptyline HCl	—	—		
Xanax see Alprazolam	—	—		

Note. From "Lethality of suicide attempt rating scale" by K. Smith, R. W. Conroy, and B. Ehler, 1984, *Suicide and Life Threatening Behavior, 14,* pp. 215–242. Copyright 1984 by Human Sciences Press. Reprinted by permission.
[a] An asterisk* indicates drugs that can be lethal with a dosage as small as 30 tablets/capsules for a 120 lb. person. These drugs are considered highly lethal.
[b] The LD$_{50}$ is the dosage or range of dosages found to kill 50% of the subjects who ingested this drug. The LD$_{50}$ numbers are in terms of milligrams of drug/kg body weight.

References

Abille v. United States, 482 F. Supp. 703 (N.D. Cal. 1980).

Addington v. Texas, 441 U.S. 418 (1979).

Afterwards, A quarterly newsletter, 5124 Grove St, Minneapolis.

Alberti, R., & Emmons, M. (1974). *Your perfect right.* San Luis Obispo, CA: Impact Press.

American Association for Marriage and Family Therapy. (n.d.). *Code of professional ethics.* Claremont, CA: Author.

American Psychiatric Association. (1987). *Diagnostic and statistical manual of mental disorders* (3rd ed., rev.). Washington, DC: Author.

American Psychiatric Association. (1981). *American Psychiatric Association. Principles of medical ethics, with annotations especially applicable to psychology.* Washington, DC: Author.

American Psychological Association. (1981). *Ethical principles for psychologists.* Washington, DC: Author.

Andress, V. R., & Corey, D. M. (1978). Survivor-victims: Who discovers or witnesses suicide? *Psychological Report, 42,* 759–764.

Ansel, E. L., & McGee, R. K. (1971). Attitudes toward suicide attempters. *Bulletin of Suicidology, 8,* 22–28.

Arffa, S. (1983). Cognition and suicide: A methodological review. *Suicide and Life-Threatening Behavior, 13,* 109–122.

Asarnow, J. R., Carlson, G. A., & Guthrie, D. (1987). Coping strategies, self-perceptions, hopelessness, and perceived family environments in depressed and suicidal children. *Journal of Consulting and Clinical Psychology, 55,* 361–366.

Barefoot v. Estelle. 463 U.S. 880, 896 (1983).

Beck, A. T., Brown, G., & Steer, R. A. (1989). Prediction of eventual suicide in psychiatric inpatients by clinical ratings of hopelessness. *Journal of Consulting and Clinical Psychology, 57,* 309–310.

Beck, A., & Emery, G. (1985). *Anxiety disorders and phobias: A cognitive perspective.* New York: Basic Book.

Beck, A. T., Kovacs, M., & Weissman, A. (1979). Assessment of suicidal ideation: The scale for suicide ideation. *Journal of Consulting and Clinical Psychology, 47,* 343–352.

Beck, A., Rush, A., Shaw, B., & Emery, G. (1979). *Cognitive therapy of depression.* New York: Guilford Press.

Beck, A. T., Schuyler, D., & Herman, I. (1974). Development of suicidal intent scales. In A. Beck, H. Resnick, & D. Lettien (Eds.), *The prediction of suicide.* Bowie, MD: The Charles Press.

Beck, A. T., Steer, R. A., Kovacs, M., & Garrison, B. (1985). Hopelessness and eventual suicide: A 10-year prospective study of patients hospitalized with suicidal ideation. *American Journal of Psychiatry, 142,* 559–563.

Beck, A. T., Weissman, A., Lester, D., & Trexler, L. (1974). The measurement of pessimism: The hopelessness scale. *Journal of Consulting and Clinical Psychology, 42,* 861–865.

Beck, J. (1987). The psychotherapist's duty to protect third parties from harm. *Mental & Physical Disabilities Law Reporter, 11,* 141–148.

Bedrosian, R. C., & Beck, A. T. (1979). Cognitive aspects of suicidal behavior. *Suicide and Life-Threatening Behavior, 9,* 87–96.

Beebe, J. E. (1975). Treatment of the suicidal patient. In C. P. Rosenbaum & J. E. Beebe (Eds.), *Psychiatric treatment: Crisis, clinic, consultation* (pp. 42–62). New York: McGraw-Hill.

Bell v. New York City Health and Hospital Corp., 90 A.D. 2d 270 (1982).

Bellah v. Greenson, 146 Cal Rptr. 535, 81 Cal App. 3d 614 (1978).

Berlin, I. (1987). Suicide among American Indian adolescents: An overview. *Suicide and Life-Threatening Behavior, 17,* 218–232.

Berman, A. L. (1975). Self-destructive behavior and suicide: Epidemiology and taxonomy. In A. R. Roberts (Ed.), *Self-destructive behavior* (pp. 5–20). Springfield, IL: Charles C Thomas.

Borkovec, T. D. (1982). Insomnia. *Journal of Consulting and Clinical Psychology, 50,* 880–895.

Brenner, M. (1973). *Mental illness and the economy.* Cambridge, MA: Harvard University Press.

Brown, J., Henteleff, P., Barakat, S., & Rowe, C. J. (1986). Is it normal for terminally ill patients to desire death? *American Journal of Psychiatry, 143,* 208–211.

Burns, D. (1980). *Feeling good.* New York: William Morrow.

Carlson, G. A., & Cantwell, D. P. (1982). Suicidal behavior and depression in children and adolescents. *Journal of the American Academy of Child Psychiatry, 21,* 361–368.

Cassidy, J., & Russo, P. (1979). Religion: A Catholic view. In L. Hankoff & B. Einsidler (Eds.), *Suicide: Theory and clinical aspects* (pp. 73–82). Littleton, MA: PSG.

Centers for Disease Control. (1985). *Suicide surveillance report: United States, 1970–1980.* Atlanta: U.S. Department of Health and Human Services.

Centers for Disease Control. (1986). *Youth suicide in the United States, 1970–1980.* Atlanta: U.S. Department of Health and Human Services.

Chemtob, C., Hamada, R., Bauer, G., Kinney, B., & Torigoe, R. (1988). Patients' suicides: Frequency and impact on psychiatrists. *American Journal of Psychiatry, 145,* 224–228.

Chemtob, M., Hamada, R., Bauer, G., Torigoe, R., & Kinney, B. (1988). Patient suicide: Frequency and impact on psychologists. *Professional Psychology: Research and Practice, 19,* 416–420.

Chiles, J. (1986). *Teenage depression and suicide.* New York: Chelsea House.

Clum, G. A., Patsiokas, A. T., & Luscomb, R. L. (1979). Empirically based comprehensive treatment program for parasuicide. *Journal of Consulting and Clinical Psychology, 47,* 937–945.

Cohen, R. J. (1979). *Malpractice. A guide for mental health professionals.* New York: The Free Press.

Cohen-Sandler, R., Berman, A. L., & King, R. (1982). A follow-up study of hospitalized suicidal children. *Journal of the American Academy of Child Psychiatry, 21,* 398–403.

Cohen-Sandler, R., & Berman, A. L. (1982, April). *Training suicidal children to problem-solve in nonsuicidal ways.* Paper presented at the annual meeting of the American Association for Suicidology, New York.

Cull, J. G., & Gill, W. S. (1982). *Suicide probability scale.* Los Angeles: Western Psychological Services.

Curran, D. K. (1987). *Adolescent Suicidal Behavior.* Washington, DC: Hemisphere Publishing Corporation.

Davis, P. A. (1983). *Suicidal adolescents.* Springfield, IL: Charles C Thomas.

Deutsch, C. J. (1984). Self-reported sources of stress among psychotherapists. *Professional Psychology, 15,* 833–845.

Diekstra, R. (1973). *A social learning theory approach to the prediction of suicidal behavior.* Paper presented at the 7th International Congress on Suicide Prevention, Amsterdam.

DiGiuseppe, R., & Miller, N. (1977). A review of outcome studies on rational-emotive therapy. In A. Ellis & R. Greiger (Eds.), *Handbook of rational-emotive therapy.* New York: Springer.

D'Zurilla, T. (1986). *Problem-solving therapy: A social competence approach to clinical intervention.* New York: Springer.

Eisenberg, L. (1984). The epidemiology of suicide in adolescents. *Pediatric Annals, 13,* 47–54.

Elkind, D. (1967). Egocentrism in adolescence. *Child Development, 38,* 1025–1034.

Ellis, A. (1962). *Reason and emotion in psychotherapy.* Seacaucus, NJ: Citadel Press.

Ellis, A. (1973). *Humanistic psychotherapy.* New York: McGraw-Hill.

Ellis, A., & Dryden, W. (1987). *The practice of rational-emotive therapy.* New York: Springer.

Ellis, T. (1986). Toward a cognitive therapy for suicidal individuals. *Professional Psychology: Theory and Research, 17,* 125–130.

Ellis, T. (1987). A cognitive approach to treating the suicidal client. In P. Keller & S. Heyman (Eds.), *Innovations in clinical practice: A source book* (Vol. 6, pp. 93–107). Sarasota, FL: Professional Resource Exchange.

Ellis, T. (1988). Classification of suicidal behavior: A review and step toward integration. *Suicide and Life-Threatening Behavior, 18,* 358–371.

Ellis, T., Berg, R., & Franzen, M. (1989, April). *Organic and cognitive deficits in suicidal patients.* Paper presented at the 22nd Annual Conference of the American Association of Suicidology, San Diego, CA.

Ellis, T., & Ratliff, K. (1986). Cognitive characteristics of suicidal and nonsuicidal psychiatric inpatients. *Cognitive Therapy and Research, 10,* 625–634.

Farber, B. A. (1983). Psychotherapists' perceptions of stressful patient behavior. *Professional Psychology: Research and Practice, 14,* 697–705.

Feindler, E. L., & Ecton, R. B. (1986). *Adolescent anger control: Cognitive-behavioral techniques.* New York: Pergamon Press.

Fingerhut, L., & Kleinman, J. (1988). Letter to the editor. *Journal of the American Medical Association, 259,* 356.

Fisher, C. R. (1988). Survivors of suicide support group surveyed. *AAS Newslink, 14,* December, p. 4.

Fishman, H. C., & Rosman, B. L. (1981). A therapeutic approach to self-destructive behavior in adolescence. The family as the patient. In C. F. Wells & I. R. Stuart (Eds.), *Self-destructive behavior in children and adolescents* (pp. 292–307). New York: Van Nostrand Reinhold.

Foster, S. L., & DeLawyer, D. D. (1987). Peer relationship problems. In R. A. Hoekelman, S. Blatman, S. B. Friedman, N. M. Nelson, & H. M. Seidel (Eds.), *Primary pediatric care.* St. Louis, MO: C V Mosby.

Fox, K., & Weissman, M. (1975). Suicide attempts and drugs: Contradiction between method and intent. *Social Psychiatry, 10,* 31–38.

Frank, J. (1973). *Persuasion and healing.* Baltimore, MD: The Johns Hopkins University Press.

Fulero, S. (1988). Tarasoff: 10 years later. *Professional Psychology: Research and Practice, 19,* 184–190.

Garner, D. M. (1986). Cognitive-behavioral therapy for eating disorders. *The Clinical Psychologist, 39,* 36–39.

Gatter, K., & Bowen, D. (1980). A study of suicide autopsies 1957–1977. *Medical Science and the Law, 20,* 37–42.

Green, A. H. (1978). Self-destructive behavior in battered children. *American Journal of Psychiatry, 135,* 579–582.

Greene, J. W., & Keown, M. (1986). Depression and suicide in children and adolescents. *Comprehensive Therapy, 12,* 38–43.

Hall, H. V. (1987). *Violence prediction.* Springfield, IL: Charles C Thomas.

Hankoff, L. (1979). Judaic origins of the suicide prohibition. In L. Hankoff & B. Einsidler (Eds.), *Suicide: Theory and clinical aspects* (pp. 3–20). Littleton, MA: PSG.

Hatton, C. L., Valente, S. M., & Rink, A. (1977). *Suicide: Assessment and intervention.* New York: Appleton-Century-Crofts.

Hawton, K. (1987). Assessment of suicide risk. *British Journal of Psychiatry, 150,* 145–153.

Hendin, H. (1982). *Suicide in America.* New York: W W Norton.

Hess, A. (1987, June). The self-imposed death sentence. *Psychology Today,* pp. 50–53.

Hogan, D. (1979). *The Regulation of Psychotherapists, 3.* Cambridge, MA: Ballinger.

Holinger (1987). *Violent deaths in the United States.* New York: Guilford Press.

Holinger, P. C., & Luke, K. W. (1984). The epidemiologic patterns of self-destructiveness in childhood, adolescence, and young adulthood. In H. S. Sudak, A. B. Ford, & N. B. Rushforth (Eds.), *Suicide in the young* (pp. 97–114). Boston: John Wright.

Holinger, P. C., & Offer, D. (1984). Toward the prediction of violent deaths among the young. In H. S. Sudak, A. B. Ford, & N. B. Rushforth (Eds.), *Suicide in the young* (pp. 15–29). Boston: John Wright.

In re Gault, 387 U.S. 1 (1967).

Joan, P. (1986). *Preventing teenage suicide: The living alternative handbook.* New York: Human Sciences Press.

Johnson v. United States. 409 F. Supp. 1283 (M.D. Fla. 1981).

Kazdin, A. E. (1988). Childhood depression. In E. J. Mash & L. O. Terdal (Eds.), *Behavioral assessment of childhood disorders* (2nd ed., pp. 157–195). New York: Guilford Press.

Kazdin, A. E., French, N. H., Unis, A. S., Esveldt-Dawson, K., & Sherick, R. B. (1983). Hopelessness, depression, and suicidal intent among psychiatrically disturbed inpatient children. *Journal of Consulting and Clinical Psychology, 51,* 504–510.

Keefe, F. J., & Ward, E. M. (1981). Behavioral approaches to the management of self-destructive children. In C. F. Wells & I. R. Stuart (Eds.), *Self-destructive behavior in children and adolescents* (pp. 309–327). New York: Van Nostrand Reinhold.

Kesey, K. (1962). *One flew over the cuckoo's nest.* New York: Signet.

Kiev, A. (1975). Psychotherapeutic strategies in the management of depressed and suicidal patients. *American Journal of Psychotherapy, 29,* 345–354.

Kleck, G. (1988). Miscounting suicides. *Suicide and Life-Threatening Behavior, 18,* 219–236.

Klein, J. I., & Glover, S. I. (1983). Psychiatric malpractice. *International Journal of Law and Psychiatry, 6,* 131–157.

Klerman, G. (1987). Clinical epidemiology of suicide. *Journal of Clinical Psychiatry, 48,* 33–38.

Koocher, G. P. (1974). Talking with children about death. *American Journal of Orthopsychiatry, 44,* 404–411.

Kreitman, N. (1977). *Parasuicide.* London: John Wiley & Sons.

Kreitman, N. (1981). The epidemiology of suicide and parasuicide. *Crisis, 2,* 1–13.

Kreitman, N. (1988). Suicide, age, and marital status. *Psychological Medicine, 18,* 121–128.

Lange, A., & Jakubowski, P. (1976). *Responsible assertive behavior: Cognitive-behavioral procedures.* Champaign, IL: Research Press.

References   155

Lazarus, A. (1984). *In the mind's eye: The power of imagery for personal enrichment.* New York: Guilford Press.

Lesse, S. (1975). The range of therapies in the treatment of severely depressed suicidal patients. *American Journal of Psychotherapy, 29,* 308–326.

Limbacher, M., & Domino, G. (1986). Attitudes toward suicide among attempters, contemplators, and nonattempters. *Omega, 16,* 325–334.

Linehan, M. (1981). A social-behavioral analysis of suicide and parasuicide: Implications for clinical assessment and treatment. In H. Glazer & J. Clarkin (Eds.), *Depression: Behavioral and directive intervention strategies* (pp. 229–294). New York: Garland.

Linehan, M. M. (1985). The reasons for living inventory. In P. Keller & L. Ritt (Eds.), *Innovations in clinical practice: A sourcebook* (pp. 321–330). Sarasota, FL: Professional Resource Exchange.

Linehan, M. (1987). Dialectical behavior therapy: A cognitive behavioral approach to parasuicide. *Journal of Personality Assessment, 1,* 328–333.

Linehan, M. M., Goodstein, J. L., Nielsen, S. L., & Chiles, J. A. (1983). Reasons for staying alive when you are thinking of killing yourself: The reasons for living inventory. *Journal of Consulting and Clinical Psychology, 51,* 276–286.

Linehan, M., & Laffaw, J. (1982). Suicidal behaviors among clients at an outpatient psychology versus the general population. *Suicide and Life-Threatening Behavior, 12,* 234–239.

Maris, R. (1981). *Pathways to suicide: A survey of self-destructive behaviors.* Baltimore: The Johns Hopkins University Press.

Maris, R. (1983). Suicide: Rights and rationality. *Suicide and Life-Threatening Behavior, 13,* 223–230.

Maris, R. (1986). *Biology of suicide.* New York: Guilford Press.

Martin, W. T. (1984). Religiosity and United States suicide rates, 1972–1978. *Journal of Clinical Psychology, 40,* 1166–1169.

Marzuk, P., Tierney, H., Tardiff, K., Gross, E., Morgan, E., Hsu, M., & Mann, J. (1988). Increased risk of suicide in persons with AIDS. *Journal of the American Medical Association, 259,* 1333–1337.

Meichenbaum, D. B. (1977). *Cognitive-behavior modification.* New York: Plenum Press.

Meichenbaum, D., & Jaremko, M. E. (1983). *Stress reduction and prevention.* New York: Plenum Press.

Meier v. Ross General Hospital, 69 Cal 2d. 420 (1968).

Miller R. D. (1985). Clinical and legal aspects of civil commitment. In C. Ewing (Ed.), *Psychology, psychiatry, and the law: A clinical and forensic handbook.* Sarasota, FL: Professional Resource Exchange.

Minkoff, K., Bergman, E., Beck, A., & Beck, R. (1973). Hopelessness, depression, and attempted suicide. *American Journal of Psychiatry, 130,* 455–459.

Mintz, R. S. (1971). Basic considerations in the psychotherapy of the depressed suicidal patient. *American Journal of Psychotherapy, 25,* 56–73.

Motto, J. A. (1977). Suicidal patients in clinical practice. *Weekly Psychiatry Update Service,* pp. 1–6.

Motto, J. A. (1988, June). Nine short-term predictors of suicide identified. *Clinical Psychiatry Newsletter,* p. 1.

Murphy, G. (1985). Suicide and attempted suicide. In R. Michels (Ed.), *Psychiatry,* (pp. 1–17). Philadelphia: J B Lippincott.

National Association of Social Workers. (1981). *Standards for the private practice of clinical social work.* Washington, DC: Author.

National Center for Health Statistics. (1988). Advance report of final mortality statistics, 1986. *Monthly vital statistics report* (Vol. 37, No. 6., Supp., DHHS Publication No. PHS 88-1120). Hyattsville, MD: Public Health Service.

National Institute of Mental Health. (1986). *Useful information on suicide*. Rockville, MD: Author.

Nelson, R. E. (1977). Irrational beliefs in depression. *Journal of Consulting and Clinical Psychology, 45,* 1190–1191.

Neuringer, C. (1976). Current developments in the study of suicidal thinking. In E. Shneidman (Ed.), *Suicidology: Contemporary developments* (pp. 234–254). New York: Grune & Stratton.

Novaco, R. W. (1977). Stress inoculation: A cognitive therapy for anger and its application to a case of depression. *Journal of Consulting and Clinical Psychology, 45,* 600–608.

O'Connor v. Donaldson, 442 U.S. 563 (1975).

Papalia, D. E., & Olds, S. W. (1986). *Human development* (3rd ed.). New York: McGraw-Hill.

Paradies v. Benedictine Hospital, 77 App. Div. 2d 757, 431 N.Y.S. 2d 175 (1980).

Patsiokas, A. T., & Clum, G. A. (1985). Effects of psychotherapeutic strategies in the treatment of suicide attempters. *Psychotherapy, 22,* 281–290.

Pattison, E., & Kahan, J. (1983). The deliberate self-harm syndrome. *American Journal of Psychiatry, 140,* 867–872.

Paykel, E. (1979). Life stress. In L. Hankoff & B. Einsidler (Eds.), *Suicide: Theory and clinical aspects* (pp. 225–234). Littleton, MA: PSG.

Pegeron, J., & Curtis, G. C. (1986). Simple phobia leading to suicide: A case report. *The Behavior Therapist, 9,* 134–135.

Perr, I. (1979). Legal aspects of suicide. In L. Hankoff & B. Einsidler (Eds.), *Suicide: Theory and clinical aspects* (pp. 91–101). Littleton, MA: PSG.

Peterson, C., & Seligman, M. E. P. (1984). Causal explanations as a risk factor for depression: Theory and evidence. *Psychological Review, 91,* 347–374.

Pfeffer, C. R. (1981). The family system of suicidal children. *American Journal of Psychotherapy, 35,* 330–341.

Pfeffer, C. R. (1984). Clinical assessment of suicidal behavior in children. In H. S. Sudak, A. B. Ford, & N. B. Rushforth (Eds.), *Suicide in the young* (pp. 171–182). Boston: John Wright.

Pfeffer, C. R. (1986). *The suicidal child.* New York: Guilford Press.

Platts, S. (1984). Unemployment and suicidal behavior: A review of the literature. *Social Science in Medicine, 19,* 93–115.

Pokorny, A. D. (1974). A scheme for classifying suicidal behaviors. In A. Beck, H. Resnik, & D. Lettien (Eds.), *The prediction of suicide* (pp. 29–44). Philadelphia, PA: The Charles Press.

Pokorny A. D. (1983). Prediction of suicide in psychiatric patients. *Archives of General Psychiatry, 40,* 249–257.

Poland, S. (1989). *Suicide intervention in the schools.* New York: Guilford Press.

Pope, K. S. (1986). New trends in malpractice cases and changes in APA liability insurance. *The Independent Practitioner, 6,* (4), 23–26.

Pope, A. W., McHale, S. M., & Craighead, W. E. (1988). *Self-esteem enhancement with children and adolescents.* New York: Pergamon Press.

Rennie v. Klein, 462 F. Supp. 1131 (1979).

Reynolds, W. (1987). *Suicide ideation questionnaire.* Odessa, FL: Psychological Assessment Resources.

Rice, E. (1973). Organic brain syndromes and suicide. *International Journal of Psychoanalytic Psychotherapy, 2,* 338–363.

Richman, J. (1981). Family treatment of suicidal children and adolescents. In C. F. Wells & I. R. Stuart (Eds.), *Self-destructive behavior in children and adolescents* (pp. 274–291). New York: Van Nostrand Reinhold.

Robbins, D. R., & Alessi, N. E. (1985). Depressive symptoms and suicidal behavior in adolescents. *American Journal of Psychiatry, 142,* 588–592.

Robins, E. (1985). Psychiatric emergency. In H. I. Kaplan and B. J. Sadok (Eds.), *Comprehensive textbook of psychiatry* (pp. 1311–1315). Baltimore: Williams & Wilkins.

Robins, E. (1986). Psychosis and suicide. *Biological Psychiatry, 21,* 665–672.

Rogers, R. (1988). *Clinical assessment of malingering and deception.* New York: Guilford Press.

Rogers v. Okin, 478 F. Supp. 1342 (1979).

Rosen, G. (1975). History. In S. Perlin (Ed.), *Handbook for the study of suicide* (pp. 3–29). New York: Oxford University Press.

Ross, C. P. (1980). Mobilizing schools for suicide prevention. *Suicide and Life-Threatening Behavior, 10,* 239–243.

Ross, C. P., & Motto, J. A. (1984). Group counseling for suicidal adolescents. In H. S. Sudak, A. B. Ford, & N. B. Rushforth (Eds.), *Suicide in the young* (pp. 367–392). Boston: John Wright.

Roy, A. (1986). Suicide in schizophrenia. In A. Roy (Ed.), *Suicide* (pp. 97–112). Baltimore: Williams & Wilkins.

Ryan, N. D., Puig-Antich, J., Ambrosini, P., Rabinovich, H., Robinson, D., Nelson, B., Iyengar, S., & Twomey, J. (1987). The clinical picture of major depression in children and adolescents. *Archives of General Psychiatry, 44,* 854–861.

Sainsbury, P. (1986). The epidemiology of suicide. In A. Roy (Ed.), *Suicide* (pp. 17–40). Baltimore: Williams & Wilkins.

Schotte, D., & Clum, G. (1987). Problem-solving skills in suicidal psychiatric patients. *Journal of Consulting and Clinical Psychology, 55,* 49–54.

Schwitzgebel, R. L., & Schwitzgebel, R. K. (1980). *Law and psychological practice.* New York: John Wiley.

Seager, C. (1986). Suicide in neurosis and personality disorder. In A. Roy (Ed.), *Suicide* (pp. 113–122). Baltimore: Williams & Wilkins.

Shaffer, D. (1974). Suicide in childhood and early adolescence. *Journal of Child Psychology and Psychiatry, 15,* 275–291.

Shaw, B., Vallis, M., & McCabe, S. (1985). The assessment of the severity and symptom patterns in depression. In E. Beckham & W. Leber (Eds.), *Handbook of depression.* Homewood, IL: Dorsey Press.

Shneidman, E. (1967, July). Recent developments in suicide prevention. *Bulletin of Suicidology,* 2–7.

Shneidman, E. (1971, June). You and death. *Psychology Today.*

Shneidman, E. (1976). Introduction: Current overview of suicide. In E. Shneidman (Ed.), *Suicidology: Contemporary developments* (pp. 1–22). New York: Grune & Stratton.

Simons, A. D., Murphy, G. E., Levine, J. L., & Wetzel, R. D. (1986). Cognitive therapy and pharmacotherapy for depression: Sustained improvement after one year. *Archives of General Psychiatry, 43,* 43–48.

Slenkovich, J. E. (Ed.) (1986, June). *The Schools' advocate.* (Available from Kinghorn Press, Inc., P. O. Box 3089, Saratoga, CA 95070).

Smith, K., Conroy, R. W., & Ehler, B. D. (1984). Lethality of suicide attempt rating scale. *Suicide and Life-Threatening Behavior, 14,* 215–242.

Smith, T. W., Houston, B. K., & Zurawski, R. W. (1984). Irrational beliefs and the arousal of emotional distress. *Journal of Counseling Psychology, 31,* 190–201.

Sorenson, S., & Golding, J. (1988). Suicide ideation and attempts in Hispanics and non-Hispanic whites: Demographic and psychiatric disorder issues. *Suicide and Life-Threatening Behavior, 18,* 205–218.

Speer v. United States, 512 F. Supp. 670 (N.D. Tex. 1981).

Spivack, G., Platt, J. J., & Shure, M. D. (1976). *The problem-solving approach to adjustment.* San Francisco: Jossey-Bass.

Suicide: Part I (1986). *Harvard Medical School Mental Health Letter, 2,* 1–4.

Suicide: An update (1986). *Statistical Bulletin, 67,* 16–23.

Suicide Research Digest. (1988). U.S. youth suicide rates, 1955–1985, 2, 1.

Survivors of Suicide Newsletter, ASS, 2459 S. Ash, Denver, CO 80222.

Szasz, T. (1986). The case against suicide prevention. *American Psychologist, 41*, 806–812.

Tarasoff in Regents of the University of California, 551 Po 2d 334, 131 Cal Rptr. 14 (Cal. Sup. Ct. 1976).

Texarkana Memorial Hospital, Inc. v. Firth, 746 S. W. 2d 494 (1988).

Thompson, R. A. (1988). Crisis intervention. In D. Capuzzi & L. Golden (Eds.), *Preventing adolescent suicide* (pp. 364–410). Muncie, IN: Accelerated Development.

Tishler, C. L., & McKenry, P. C. (1982). Parental negative self and adolescent suicide attempts. *Journal of the American Academy of Child Psychiatry, 21*, 404–408.

Topel v. Long Island Jewish Medical Center. 431 N.E. 2d 293 (1981).

Trexler, L. (1973). The suicidal person and the restoration of hope. *Rational Living, 8*, 19–23.

Turk, D., Meichenbaum, D., & Genest, M. (1983). *Pain and behavioral medicine.* New York: Guilford Press.

Turkington, C. (1986, November). Suit data show no need to panic. *APA Monitor, 9.*

United States monthly vital statistics (1984). Vol. 33.

Walen, S. R., DiGiuseppe, R., & Wessler, R. L. (1980). *A practitioner's guide to rational-emotive therapy.* New York: Oxford University Press.

Weissman, A., & Worden, J. (1972). Risk-rescue rating in suicide assessment. *Archives of General Psychiatry, 26*, 553–560.

Westefeld, J. & Furr, S. (1987). Suicide and depression among college students. *Professional Psychology: Research and Practice, 18*, 119–123.

Whitlock, F. A. (1982). The neurology of affective disorder and suicide. *Australian and New Zealand Journal of Psychiatry, 16*, 1–12.

Whitlock, F. (1986). Suicide and physical illness. In A. Roy (Ed.), *Suicide* (pp. 151–170). Baltimore: Williams & Wilkins.

Williams, C. B., & Nickels, J. B. (1969). Internal-external control dimensions as related to accident and suicide proneness. *Journal of Consulting and Clinical Psychology, 33*, 485–494.

Wright, J. H., & Beck, A. T. (1983). Cognitive therapy of depression: Theory and practice. *Hospital and Community Psychiatry, 34*, 1119–1127.

Wyatt v. Stickney, 325 F. Supp. 781 (1971).

Youth suicide rates: 1955–1985 (1988). *Suicide Research Digest, 2*, 1.

Author Index

Subject Index

ABOUT THE AUTHORS

William J. Fremouw, PhD, is currently Professor of Psychology at West Virginia University where he is the Director of Clinical Training. Dr. Fremouw received his PhD from the University of Massachusetts in 1974 and completed his internship at the University of Rochester Medical Center in 1975. He is a diplomate in forensic psychology from the American Board of Professional Psychology. His current interests are forensic psychology, eating disorders, and anxiety disorders. He has published numerous articles in scientific journals and is editor of three other books.

Maria de Perczel, MA, received her degree in Behavior Analysis and Therapy from Southern Illinois University in 1985. A doctoral student in Child Clinical Psychology at West Virginia University, she is currently completing her internship at the Florida Mental Health Institute at the University of South Florida. Her research interests involve child abuse and neglect, with particular emphasis on the etiology and treatment of child and adolescent psychopathology.

Thomas E. Ellis, PsyD, is Associate Professor of Psychology at the Department of Behavioral Medicine and Psychiatry of the West Virginia University (WVU) Health Sciences Center (Charleston Division). He received his bachelor's degree from the University of Texas and his doctorate from Baylor University. He pursued postdoctoral training at the Institute for Rational-Emotive Therapy in New York City, where he is an Associate Fellow and Supervisor. His research interests are on cognitive aspects of suicide and the classification of suicidal behavior. In addition to his clinical work, he teaches cognitive-behavior therapy to psychology interns and psychiatry residents and is codirector of the WVU Panic Disorder Clinic.

Psychology Practitioner Guidebooks

Editors
Arnold P. Goldstein, Syracuse University
Leonard Krasner, Stanford University & SUNY at Stony Brook
Sol L. Garfield, Washington University in St. Louis

Elsie M. Pinkston & Nathan L. Linsk—CARE OF THE ELDERLY:
A Family Approach

Donald Meichenbaum—STRESS INOCULATION TRAINING

Sebastiano Santostefano—COGNITIVE CONTROL THERAPY WITH
CHILDREN AND ADOLESCENTS

Lillie Weiss, Melanie Katzman & Sharlene Wolchik—TREATING BULIMIA:
A Psychoeducational Approach

Edward B. Blanchard & Frank Andrasik—MANAGEMENT OF CHRONIC
HEADACHES: A Psychological Approach

Raymond G. Romanczyk—CLINICAL UTILIZATION OF
MICROCOMPUTER TECHNOLOGY

Philip H. Bornstein & Marcy T. Bornstein—MARITAL THERAPY:
A Behavioral-Communications Approach

Michael T. Nietzel & Ronald C. Dillehay—PSYCHOLOGICAL
CONSULTATION IN THE COURTROOM

Elizabeth B. Yost, Larry E. Beutler, M. Anne Corbishley & James R.
Allender—GROUP COGNITIVE THERAPY: A Treatment Approach for
Depressed Older Adults

Lillie Weiss—DREAM ANALYSIS IN PSYCHOTHERAPY

Edward A. Kirby & Liam K. Grimley—UNDERSTANDING AND
TREATING ATTENTION DEFICIT DISORDER

Jon Eisenson—LANGUAGE AND SPEECH DISORDERS IN CHILDREN

Eva L. Feindler & Randolph B. Ecton—ADOLESCENT ANGER
CONTROL: Cognitive-Behavioral Techniques

Michael C. Roberts—PEDIATRIC PSYCHOLOGY: Psychological
Interventions and Strategies for Pediatric Problems

Daniel S. Kirschenbaum, William G. Johnson & Peter M. Stalonas, Jr.—
TREATING CHILDHOOD AND ADOLESCENT OBESITY

W. Stewart Agras—EATING DISORDERS: Management of Obesity,
Bulimia and Anorexia Nervosa

Ian H. Gotlib & Catherine A. Colby—TREATMENT OF DEPRESSION:
An Interpersonal Systems Approach

Walter B. Pryzwansky & Robert N. Wendt—PSYCHOLOGY AS A
PROFESSION: Foundations of Practice

Cynthia D. Belar, William W. Deardorff & Karen E. Kelly—THE
PRACTICE OF CLINICAL HEALTH PSYCHOLOGY

Paul Karoly & Mark P. Jensen—MULTIMETHOD ASSESSMENT OF
CHRONIC PAIN

William L. Golden, E. Thomas Dowd & Fred Friedberg—
HYPNOTHERAPY: A Modern Approach

Patricia Lacks—BEHAVIORAL TREATMENT FOR PERSISTENT INSOMNIA

Arnold P. Goldstein & Harold Keller—AGGRESSIVE BEHAVIOR:
Assessment and Intervention

C. Eugene Walker, Barbara L. Bonner & Keith L. Kaufman—
THE PHYSICALLY AND SEXUALLY ABUSED CHILD: Evaluation
and Treatment

Robert E. Becker, Richard G. Heimberg & Alan S. Bellack—SOCIAL
SKILLS TRAINING TREATMENT FOR DEPRESSION

Richard F. Dangel & Richard A. Polster—TEACHING CHILD
MANAGEMENT SKILLS

Albert Ellis, John F. McInerney, Raymond DiGiuseppe & Raymond
Yeager—RATIONAL-EMOTIVE THERAPY WITH ALCOHOLICS
AND SUBSTANCE ABUSERS

Johnny L. Matson & Thomas H. Ollendick—ENHANCING CHILDREN'S
SOCIAL SKILLS: Assessment and Training

Edward B. Blanchard, John E. Martin & Patricia M. Dubbert—NON-DRUG
TREATMENTS FOR ESSENTIAL HYPERTENSION

Samuel M. Turner & Deborah C. Beidel—TREATING OBSESSIVE-
COMPULSIVE DISORDER

Alice W. Pope, Susan M. McHale & W. Edward Craighead—SELF-
ESTEEM ENHANCEMENT WITH CHILDREN AND ADOLESCENTS

Jean E. Rhodes & Leonard A. Jason—PREVENTING SUBSTANCE
ABUSE AMONG CHILDREN AND ADOLESCENTS

Gerald D. Oster, Janice E. Caro, Daniel R. Eagen & Margaret A. Lillo—
ASSESSING ADOLESCENTS

Robin C. Winkler, Dirck W. Brown, Margaret van Keppel & Amy
Blanchard—CLINICAL PRACTICE IN ADOPTION

Roger Poppen—BEHAVIORAL RELAXATION TRAINING AND
ASSESSMENT

Michael D. LeBow—ADULT OBESITY THERAPY

Robert Paul Liberman, William J. DeRisi & Kim T. Mueser—SOCIAL
SKILLS TRAINING FOR PSYCHIATRIC PATIENTS

Johnny L. Matson—TREATING DEPRESSION IN CHILDREN AND
ADOLESCENTS

Sol L. Garfield—THE PRACTICE OF BRIEF PSYCHOTHERAPY

Arnold P. Goldstein, Barry Glick, Mary Jane Irwin,
Claudia Pask-McCartney & Ibrahim Rubama—REDUCING
DELINQUENCY: Intervention in the Community

Albert Ellis, Joyce L. Sichel, Raymond J. Yeager, Dominic J. DiMattia &
Raymond DiGiuseppe—RATIONAL-EMOTIVE COUPLES THERAPY

Clive R. Hollin—COGNITIVE-BEHAVIORAL INTERVENTIONS WITH
YOUNG OFFENDERS

Margaret P. Korb, Jeffrey Gorrell & Vernon Van De Riet—GESTALT
THERAPY: Practice and Theory, Second Edition

Donald A. Williamson—ASSESSMENT OF EATING DISORDERS
Obesity, Anorexia, and Bulimia Nervosa